REST FOR THE WEARY

Shay S. Mason

LVE

INSIDE OUT

Copyright ©2021 by Shay S. Mason
Published by LIO Press
9650 Strickland Rd.
Suite 103-401
Raleigh, NC 27615
www.loveinsideout.org

Printed in the United States of America

ISBN: 978-1-7365715-0-7 (Paperback)
ISBN: 978-1-7365715-1-4 (eBook)

Edited by Nina Hundley. Cover design by Abi Partridge. Interior design by Tom Carroll. Author photo by Avery Mason.

CONTENTS

For all who have fought valiantly against fear.

I sought the Lord, and he answered me; he delivered me from all my fears.

— PSALM 34:4

ACKNOWLEDGEMENTS

This book is the product of many years of seeking and searching, longing and learning. I am grateful to all those who have walked beside me in the journey. First, I must thank my husband Bruce for always being my strongest advocate and cheerleader as well as a tireless editor. Gratitude is due to my family for patiently bearing with me as I struggled to build a platform and find my voice. I must also thank my Fatherheart family for helping me discover my true identity and find the courage to live from that place. I am particularly indebted to Denise Jordan for her gracious foreword to this book. Additionally, the Hope*Writer community has been an invaluable resource as I've learned the ins and outs of putting an idea into print. Finally, huge thanks to everyone who provided valuable content insight, formatting help, graphic design, and editing assistance along the way — especially Bruce, Lisa, Lauren, Mark, Grace, Rosa, Nina, Abi, and Tom. I couldn't have done it without you.

FOREWORD

Jesus said, "Come to me, all you who are weary and burdened, and I will give you rest" (Matthew 11:28). Did we ever really believe how much we needed rest? He could have said many things: I will give you joy, I will give you peace, I will give you eternal life? These are all true but not what Jesus was revealing to us at this point.

I often think of how our Heavenly Father was looking at the human race down the years and seeing the pain and confusion about who he is. All the striving, wars, fear, and superstition about who this God is. Is he loving, scary, angry, vengeful?

Generation after generation wondered, pondered and, for the most part, concluded that God is a hard master who demands perfection and sacrifice. He loves who he will love and hates who he will hate. This is a God that it is best to keep our distance from.

Yet, the Bible says, "When the time had fully come, God sent his Son" (Galatians 4:4). He sent his Son to once and for all reveal to the human race what he (the Father) is really like.

Now we know—God the father is just like Jesus. He came in weakness, vulnerability, and humility. He came to reveal what God is truly like. He came to give rest to the humble — those who are humble enough to receive it.

Yes, I say, "humble enough" because it took humility to finally admit that all my trying, all my praying, all my fasting, and all my doing had not brought me into the deep intimacy with God that I longed for. And yet, I still wondered if I had done enough, been loving enough, sacrificed enough, had faith enough ... the list is endless.

In my early years of trying to walk with God, I remember reading where Jesus said, "Unless your righteousness exceeds the righteousness of the Pharisees and teachers of the law you will certainly not enter the Kingdom of Heaven" (Matthew 5:20). Wow! That put what I then called "the fear of God" into me.

How would I ever attain to that? In my desire to know God, I gave it everything I had. After twenty years, I had finally come to spiritual and emotional exhaustion and failure.

I came to find that failure was my friend. When all my efforts fell to the ground, and I could no longer lift my head up—when I had no more inclination to help another soul, another world opened to me.

I found Love. Love, compassion, mercy, and faithfulness, which led me into rest.

The righteousness that exceeds that of the Pharisees is superseded by the love that Jesus came to reveal. The love, originating in the Father's heart, that so loved the world. The love that Paul says is long and high and wide and deep. Love that is greater than we could ever comprehend.

It is the love that created this beautiful world.

It is the love that causes the sun to rise each day.

It is the love that causes the rain to fall on the righteous and the unrighteous.

It is the same love that gives grace to the humble and rest to those who are weary from trying to do what's right and good.

It is the love so big it loves its enemies.

This love does not keep a record of mistakes or even deliberate wrongs. This love can wait for you, teach you to listen, and remain patient while you learn.

Jesus said, "Be perfect even as your Heavenly Father is perfect" (Matthew 5:48). Again, this seems so unattainable. Interestingly, that word "perfect" can also be translated as "whole." The paradox is that in God's upside-down world, wholeness comes to us through failure as we humble ourselves and confess our need to be led.

Wholeness comes by allowing him to heal our hearts, our deepest wounds, of all pain, fear and anguish.

In this book, Shay opens her heart wide. She lets you into the dark places of her heart where light has come in. If you have a need for a miracle, follow the wisdom that has been hard-won. In doing so, it will lead you to the wholeness that will answer your deepest need—the need to know the love that leads your heart into rest.

– Denise Jordan
Co-founder - Fatherheart Ministries

INTRODUCTION

The Ugly Weed

My struggle with fear began when I was just four years old. My friend Sarah had convinced me to explore a stairway she discovered in the Methodist Church where we attended preschool. I wasn't so sure about this plan, but Sarah was already five, therefore older and wiser. We went together up the winding stone staircase and came out in a dark, cold room made of the same rough stone. I looked to my right and saw something I'd never seen before: death.

I don't know how long I stared at the woman in the casket. I did not know who she was, but I was certain I was looking at someone who was dead. We weren't supposed to be there, and I immediately felt the sting of shame. My heart pounded and my feet froze. I'd made a bad decision, and I believed this was my punishment.

After a few moments, Sarah and I ran back down the staircase as fast as our little legs would carry us. We returned to our classroom huffing and puffing. Our teachers were none the wiser, and we agreed never to tell anyone what we had done. We went about our morning playing on rainbow-colored rugs with our favorite Fisher-Price toys as if nothing had happened.

I don't remember ever speaking with Sarah about it again. And I told no one about the woman in the casket until many years later during prayer ministry. But I believe a seed was planted that day, and it grew into a pretty nasty weed—one I did not know how to kill. From that moment forward, anything related to death felt shameful and terrifying. I couldn't talk about it with my parents, even when my grandmother died three years later.

My grandmother's death was unexpected. She was only in her fifties and had died in her sleep. I remember crying when I found out, but I quickly bottled up my questions and anxiety. At night, I would lie in bed terrified I wouldn't wake up in the morning. I think I said something to my mother about my fear one night, and she assured me I would be okay. Yet the fears lingered.

Fear wasn't a constant part of my life when I was young, but it would sometimes rear its unwelcome head when I was sick with something that seemed more serious than a typical childhood illness. Migraines convinced me I had a brain tumor. Getting my adenoids removed meant I might not wake up from the anesthesia. Still, I rarely voiced my fears and the ugly weed continued to grow.

When I was twelve, we received a call that a friend of mine had been diagnosed with cancer. A cold fear hit me. I didn't want to ask questions that might produce an answer I didn't want to hear. I only remember running out of the house and down a path into the woods where I could be alone. I sat by myself and cried. Although I wasn't raised in a Christian home, I'm pretty sure I talked to God. I wanted some assurance that my friend wouldn't die. I needed to know that someone was with me in my fear.

Around this same time, I also started to display obsessive-compulsive behavior. My father was a police officer who always worked Friday nights. From the time I was school age, my mom and I would enjoy a girls' night on Fridays. We would often go somewhere fun for dinner, then do a little shopping. We tried to get home in time for the popular Friday night television show of the era, *Dallas*. Mom and I needed to know who shot J. R. of course.

I remember sitting in our family room watching TV with a restlessness that was driven solely by fear, and not about J. R. Ewing. I knew Friday nights could be dangerous for a police officer, and I was always afraid my dad wouldn't come home. So I would sit on the sofa and try to watch the show, feeling compelled to go to the window every ten minutes and make sure no police car had arrived to deliver dreaded news. I came up with an excuse each time I got up: "Just grabbing a snack" or "Where did the cat go?" I knew this compulsion was abnormal, and it didn't really accomplish anything. It's not as if I could protect my dad by looking out the window. As I peered into the darkness, my heart would pound every time a car came down the road. I would wait for it to pass, then go back to the family room. My fears would not subside until I heard the garage door open well after midnight.

This is how I experienced nearly every Friday night for years.

From high school into the beginning of college, I went through a rough time. During those years, I lost two friends and two grandparents. I didn't hide from what was going on. I went to the funerals, and even sang at two of them, but I remember feeling empty. I wanted to share my grief with others, but I didn't know how. It felt like something shameful clung to me.

The funeral of my sixteen-year-old friend who had died in a car accident was at the same time as a rehearsal for an important choir concert. I told the director I felt it was important to attend the funeral and shared that I had been asked to sing with a small group from school. Her response was sharp. "There is no excuse for missing this rehearsal. People die and you need to accept that. I am disappointed that you would even ask." Shame flooded over me. I went out to my car and cried until I ran out of tears. In that moment, I could not see how this event played into my feelings of shame and fear. But a year later, when the choir director lost her job because of emotional abuse accusations brought forward by several parents, I reflected on how her words had affected me.

One obvious manifestation was my growing need to be the perfect chorister and prove my commitment to her. It no longer mattered if I had a fever of 103 or a limb dangling precariously from its socket, I would be at choir rehearsal with a smile on my face. And this level of commitment continued even after her removal. Of course, dedication is an admirable trait, but not when it's driven by fear and a need to control circumstances. There is no freedom in the commitment that seeks only to please others or avoid punishment. This lesson took me years to learn.

I became a Christian during college when I was nineteen. As someone with a long history of living from my head, I had not imagined this would be part of my college experience. Like many young people, I thought I had life all figured out. I was involved in a sorority, music ensembles, political organizations, and student government. My life felt full, and I had zero inclination toward any of the "spiritual" groups on campus.

So it came as a shock one evening when I walked into a Bible study and gave my life to Christ within five minutes. I honestly had no idea what I had done. I'd gone to the meeting just to get someone to stop asking me to check it out. Upon arrival, I realized it was a Jesus ambush. They were clearly waiting for me and wasted no time asking if I wanted to accept Jesus as my Lord and Savior. To my utter surprise, I stepped forward and said, "Yes!" It felt as if someone had pushed me forward from the center of my back when, in reality, no one was behind me. The word just shot out of my mouth. My mind actively protested this move, but my heart was stirred by something I didn't understand. It would be years before I could understand the move of the Spirit that took place in my heart that night.

I knew something important had happened, but I didn't have any framework for it. I didn't know what living as a Christian actually meant, but I prayed I would know in my heart I had been changed.

It would be nice to say all my fears disappeared as I was overcome by some blessed assurance, but that was not the case. There would be many more mountains and valleys (along with the occasional avalanche and flood) on the journey, but sometimes ignorance is bliss. Fear of death continued to be a significant source of unease for me, but there are many other things that cause fear, and I dealt with a myriad of them. Fear of death led to fear of illness. Fear of illness led to fear of doctors' appointments and hospitals. And don't even get me started on all the fears that crept in after I had children. I'll get to those later. Suffice it to say, even after becoming a Christian, the ugly weed was alive and well.

I know there are people who have had a much closer walk with death. At this point in my life, I haven't lost a parent, a spouse, or child, nor have I experienced a battle with cancer. But the enemy still exploited my past experiences to nurture the shame and fear planted in my heart. Without even realizing it, I walked many miles of this journey with a disconnect between my head and my heart. I knew something was wrong, but I didn't know what. Perhaps the worst part was that because my fears didn't go away, I also began to fear that I wasn't saved—or worse, that I *couldn't* be saved. The enemy had me right where he wanted me: believing I didn't even belong to God. And when we don't know who or *whose* we are, we feel powerless.

If you feel like fear is consuming you, I promise you there is a way out. If you are tired of battling for control of your mind, be encouraged. You have a loving Father who wants to bring you into a spacious place, and his perfect love really does cast out fear. If you are fighting the desire to surrender, stop fighting. Wave your white flag right where you are and let the one who loves you most meet you in that surrender. Think about how Henri Nouwen describes it: "God, creator of heaven and earth, has chosen to be, first and foremost, a Father."[1] And he is your Father.

This book is less of a "how-to" and more of an invitation to begin a journey of restoration to the heart of your loving Father, where fear simply cannot stand. He is a good gardener and able to uproot even the most noxious of weeds. Are you willing to rest and let him cultivate love in your heart?

CHAPTER 1

HEAD VERSUS HEART

"Keep vigilant watch over your heart; that's where life starts."

— PROVERBS 4:23 *(THE MESSAGE)*

Fear is primarily a problem of the heart, not the head. While our heads are undoubtedly involved, the root of fear is found in our broken hearts—hearts that have not encountered the fullness of God's love. We see our own failures: all the times we haven't acted in love, wouldn't forgive, became impatient, or succumbed to rage or lust. Deep down, many of us believe we deserve to be punished because we know we are broken, flawed, and unable to fix ourselves. We ask ourselves, *Can God really love me? How can I love him the way I should?*

We know from 1 John 4:19 that "we love because he first loved us." What a relief! It's not about trying harder to love. It's about receiving his unconditional love. Sadly, we often don't know how to receive that love. Most of us are wired for busyness. We believe we'll find intimacy with God by serving more, praying harder, or reading the Bible longer, but what our hearts truly long for is rest. Only in a posture of rest can we receive all the love he has for us.

Our hearts have become detached from the source of joy and peace, and in that state of detachment, the mind tries to take control. If you're like me, you've realized the mind is not so trustworthy. I would convince myself one minute that I had my fear under control (while patting myself of the back for being a "good Christian,") and the next moment I'd find myself caught in a wave of self-condemnation, doubt, or complete panic. The mind is a tricky thing, but what can be done?

Paul gives us an answer in Ephesians 3:16-18: "I pray that out of his glorious riches he may strengthen you with power through his Spirit in your inner being, so that Christ may dwell in your hearts through faith. And I pray that you, being rooted and established in love, may have power, together with all the Lord's holy people, to grasp how wide and long and high and deep is the love of Christ."

Being rooted and established in love is where it all begins. The attainment of this condition must occur in the heart, because that is where God desires to dwell. Take a moment and ponder this: the Creator of the universe wants to make *his* home in *your* heart. He gives us access to all that is his. When his love has taken root in our heart, true understanding is unleashed and faith flourishes.

Proverbs 4:23 gives insight into the very real importance of the heart. "Keep your heart with all vigilance, for from it flow the springs of life" (ESV). When these springs get clogged up with the debris of our brokenness, love cannot flow freely. Real transformation flows from love, not the other way around. We can't transform ourselves to produce love. God's love alone is what creates lasting change. If we don't receive his love, we don't change. And if we have a blockage, receiving his love can be difficult.

Not only are we called to be filled with his love, Jesus also tells us to abide in it (John 15:9). The Greek word used here is *meinate*. It is the imperative form of *meno,* meaning to remain, stay, or dwell continuously. We are not supposed to dip into his love from time to time; we are commanded to live in it. His love is our true home. And he is the one who makes it possible by imparting this very love into our hearts. This is the key to transformation. As God makes his home in our hearts, we are invited to dwell in his. What a marvelous mystery! Henri Nouwen wrote, "We are speaking here about a mystery for which words are inadequate. It is the mystery that the heart, which is the center of our being, is transformed by God into his own heart, a heart large enough to embrace the entire universe."[1]

Allowing God's love to penetrate the darkest areas of our hearts is crucial. It is only then that our minds can be renewed. The deepest truth I have come to understand throughout my journey is stated in 1 John 4:18: "There is no fear in love, but perfect love casts out fear. For fear has to do with punishment, and whoever fears has not been perfected in love" (ESV). It is the substance of God's love that banishes fear, not our own positive thinking or willpower. There is nothing we can do with our minds to cause this transformation to take place. Love must be received in the heart, but this can be difficult when our hearts are battered, bruised, and scarred. There is no one who wants to see your heart healed more than God, and you can trust him to lead you through the process. As C. S. Lewis wrote, "Give me All [of yourself] . . . I will give you a new self instead. In fact, I will give you Myself: my own will shall become yours."[2] When he imparts his nature to us, that includes his heart and all it holds.

☙

Early in my twenties, fear took on a different and even more troubling dimension. As I mentioned in my introduction, because my fear of death was not replaced by a deep assurance of salvation after I accepted Christ, I feared I was not saved. At twenty-three, and still relatively new to Christianity, I married someone who had recently returned to faith. At first, we felt like we were really walking in faith together. But my husband never seemed to struggle with doubts, so I started believing there was something seriously wrong with me.

I went to Christian conferences and retreats, hoping someone could assure me of my salvation. I scoured the book table at these events, looking for something that might hold the answer. Expecting to find peace, I would read scripture but get hung up on the parable of the sower in Matthew 13:1-23. *What if my heart was just bad soil?* Other times, I would become bothered by the parable of the weeds in Matthew 13:24-30. *I must be a weed!*

On the outside, I looked like a good Christian wife, music ministry leader, and Bible study teacher. On the inside, I was screaming for some proof that all the promises of God actually applied to me. Could God truly be that good?

Perhaps this resonates with you.

Some years later, when I first shared my struggle with doubt to a group of mature Christians, I wondered how it would be received. Would I be judged? Would I be deemed unworthy of leadership? Would they simply have no idea what I was talking about? To my surprise, none of these things happened. Instead, several people approached me saying they'd never heard anyone share so honestly about fear and doubt. This had been their story as well, and they had often thought they were alone in their struggle.

If this is you, be assured you are not alone. God is with you, even in your fear and doubts, and he is not condemning you. He longs to pour more of his love into you and see you step free from your chains.

During our early years of marriage, my husband became ill

with debilitating food allergies. He had struggled with allergies for much of his life, but suddenly the bottom dropped out. Foods that had previously been safe began causing a vast array of unpleasant symptoms, from drastic mood swings to boils. He became allergic to just about every food you could imagine and was subjected to a diet comprising African roots, plain tapioca noodles, and rabbit. He went to great lengths to find food that wasn't toxic to him. (For the record, don't try rattlesnake. There's a reason you probably won't find it on the menu at a Michelin-starred restaurant—or anywhere else.)

From our peculiar culinary adventures to experimental, and often unpleasant, medical treatments, that time in our lives was a challenge. My husband was slowly wasting away before my eyes. He weighed less than I did, and I could see all his ribs. His digestive system was failing, and he experienced distressing cardiac symptoms. We could no longer do the things we loved to do together. Enjoying a fine restaurant was out of the question, and so were weekend hiking trips. Bruce spent each day just trying to survive. We were desperate, but it had never occurred to either of us that God could heal him. That just wasn't part of our church background.

After moving to Washington, D. C., we joined a church that had a vibrant prayer ministry. Not long after we started attending, the church announced a healing event led by a guest speaker from Australia. We were curious because people spoke so highly of this Australian, but we went with few expectations. Little did we know, that event led by a humble, elderly

Anglican priest from Sydney would change our lives in ways we could never imagine. It was then we first realized we have a God who heals. Not just a God who healed some people a long time ago, but a God who heals *today*. My husband has a remarkable healing testimony of his own. Through the love and commitment of a couple involved in the prayer ministry at our church, Bruce received incredible heart healing, which ultimately resulted in freedom from his allergies. But it was also through the love of this couple that I first understood the importance of the heart.

When Bruce and I first met Lynn and Bill, we merely wanted prayer for his allergies. We thought we would explain Bruce's problem, and they would pray with us asking God to heal him. It seemed pretty straightforward to us. But when they asked questions about his background—"What was your relationship like with your parents?" and "When did you find out you were adopted?"—we knew we had stepped into a different kind of journey. Bruce was being led deep into identity-related heart wounds he didn't even know he had.

I learned so much as I walked with my husband on that journey. It was like watching someone go through heart surgery. We knew it had to happen. We prayed the outcome would be good, but the process was painful. Months went by and Lynn and Bill continued to pray with us. Sometimes we'd feel like we were seeing breakthrough, but Bruce's health continued to decline. Throughout the process, Lynn faithfully reminded us that God was doing this in his time. He knew what Bruce needed, and he knew the best order and pace to proceed. It took many months, but when the healing came, it was dramatic.

During this time, I knew God was telling me I needed this kind of heart work too. But I could always rationalize myself out of it. I wasn't sick like Bruce. I wasn't adopted, as Bruce had been, so I didn't struggle with the same identity issues. My career was going well. If I ignored the underlying anxiety, things seemed okay on my end. I just wanted to see my husband healed. But the enemy knew how much I needed healing, even if I didn't. And he knows how to exploit our fears to keep us from finding freedom.

One evening, we'd had a powerful prayer time with Bill and Lynn. It felt like a real breakthrough for Bruce, and we left the house in an optimistic mood. As we walked down the path across Bill and Lynn's well-manicured suburban lawn, I halted in terror. A large black snake slithered across the path, just inches from my foot. I am a lover of nature, but if there's one thing in all creation that terrifies me, it's snakes. I believe the enemy knew that. I froze in the center of the lawn and screamed. If any of the neighbors were watching, it must have been quite a sight. Once I caught my breath, I ran like a madwoman to our Jeep parked on the other side of the road.

Bruce had no idea what had happened. I jumped in the car, still panting, and gasped, "Snake!" Bruce hadn't seen a thing, but I was sure that nasty serpent was real. As we drove home,

I called Lynn and told her what I'd seen. She was perplexed. They'd lived in that house for many years and had never once seen a snake. Fear and doubt took hold of my heart. *Was I crazy?*

When I look back, I realize I gave the enemy a foothold that day. For some time, I wanted little to do with healing prayer. Real or not, if Satan shows up to terrorize you after a breakthrough, I didn't want any part of it. So, I continued to hide from my fears and any chance of healing.

I also persisted in an unhealthy pattern of self-judgment. My blindness to God's love even caused me to use scripture as a tool for condemnation. James 1:6-8 convinced me that because I struggled with doubt I shouldn't expect God to help me. "But when you ask, you must believe and not doubt, because the one who doubts is like a wave of the sea, blown and tossed by the wind. That person should not expect to receive anything from the Lord. Such a person is double-minded and unstable in all they do." My wounded heart perceived only judgment in this passage.

Certainly, I was caught in a state of double-mindedness at that point in my life, but I accepted the words to such an extent that I wallowed in unworthiness. All I could see was my instability and failure to control my thoughts. I didn't know how to fix my mind, so I figured God wouldn't answer my prayers. And because my mind was in chaos, I didn't think my heart could receive anything. How wrong I was!

As I watched Bruce, I discovered the importance of the heart in spiritual, emotional, and physical well-being. I knew my heart had a problem, but I wasn't sure I wanted to walk through the pain of spiritual heart surgery. The enemy sure didn't want me to deal with my heart, so he kept me trapped in my mind. I questioned my identity in Christ and the goodness of God. I questioned whether God could heal. I questioned whether God could heal *me*. The questions kept coming. Despite my attempts to fill my mind with God's truth, peace eluded me.

As Christians, we are often taught the truth we receive in our minds will eventually reach our heart. This certainly has not been my experience, and if you're reading this book, I suspect it hasn't been yours either. We declare God's Word; we proclaim his truth over our situation, and we wait in expectation. And none of these things are wrong, but our declarations will not be a catalyst for change if we don't give God access to our heart. Constantly doing battle against your own mind is tiring. It feels like a battle you can't ever win—and you can't win it on your own. You have a God who is victorious, and his victory starts with a heart at rest. I want to show you, as Paul would say, a more excellent way to find your freedom. It starts with love.

Questions for Reflection

1. Where do you struggle with condemnation in your life?

2. How do you think God sees you? What do you look like through his eyes of love?

3. Have there been times when you've avoided a healing encounter with God? What were your reasons? Ask God to show you his perspective.

Going Deeper

Sit for a few moments and ask God to show you a place, real or imaginary, where he would like to meet with you. What did he show you or say to you? Close your eyes and meet him there. **Suggestion: Journal or draw what he shows you.**

Therefore, there is now no condemnation for those who are in Christ Jesus...

— ROMANS 8:1

CHAPTER 2

THE EYES OF THE HEART

"It is very simple: It is only with the heart that one can see rightly; what is essential is invisible to the eye."

— ANTOINE DE SAINT-EXUPÉRY,
THE LITTLE PRINCE

One of our most important resources for confronting fear is the Word of God. Romans 12:2 reminds us not to "conform to the pattern of this world, but be transformed by the renewing of your mind." As a person struggling with fear, this became my constant refrain. I memorized helpful scripture. I wrote it on note cards and carried them in my purse, my pocket, and the car. One of my favorites was 2 Timothy 1:7, which I liked to quote from the New King James Version: "For God has not given us a spirit of fear, but of power and of love and of a sound mind." It's a great verse to hold on to when you're struggling with fear, right? But my problem was how I berated myself with it while I tried to force my mind to believe it. I told myself if I just kept repeating verses like this, I would eventually experience the sought-after renewing of my mind. So I clung to my verses while both my heart and mind remained virtually unchanged.

Over time, as I became frustrated at the lack of change, I blamed myself. Why couldn't I just get rid of my fearful thoughts by trusting in God's Word? Did I not have enough faith? Why didn't God's truth enter my head and drop to my heart the way I was told it should?

Again, I returned to the parable of the sower. Every moment, it seemed my faith was being choked by the cares of the world, just like the person described in Matthew 13:7. The thorns were everywhere. But I'd tried to defeat the thorns. I'd tried so hard, and I wasn't winning the battle. My heart sure seemed like bad soil.

But what I hadn't noticed was something quite profound, staring at me from the passage that seemed to condemn me. Right in the middle of the parable of the sower, Jesus quotes from the prophet Isaiah:

You will be ever hearing but never understanding;
you will be ever seeing but never perceiving.
For this people's heart has become calloused;
they hardly hear with their ears,
and they have closed their eyes.
Otherwise, they might see with their eyes,

hear with their ears,
understand with their hearts
and turn, and I would heal them.

– MATTHEW 13:14-15

For years, I had struggled to figure out the difference between knowledge and understanding. I thought if I could put as much scripture in my head as possible and wield it as a weapon when needed, I could win the battle. But that remedy relies on head knowledge and willpower. Retaining scriptural knowledge wasn't a problem for me, but in beating back fear, my will was weak. I truly was "like a wave of the sea, blown and tossed by the wind" (James 1:6).

What Jesus wants us to grasp is that knowing truth in our head is not the same as understanding it in our hearts. Think of the Pharisees. They knew scripture and could quote whole passages with ease, but their hearts didn't understand the true meaning, as confirmed by their lack of love. Just two chapters after the parable of the sower, in Matthew 15:7-9, we find Jesus strongly rebuking the Pharisees:

You hypocrites! Isaiah was right when he prophesied about you:

'These people honor me with their lips,
but their hearts are far from me.
They worship me in vain;
their teachings are merely human rules.'

Three verses later, he describes them as "blind guides." Jesus knew the eyes of their hearts were closed.

When we truly understand the immensity of God's love for us and receive it in our heart, he heals us while redirecting and strengthening our will. Our hearts become open to all that is possible. I love what James Jordan of Fatherheart Ministries says about this: "Love changes you into everything that God has ever intended you to be."[1] God's love opens the eyes of our hearts to his most profound truths and satisfies our deepest needs. Kingdom perspective becomes reality.

Sadly, for many of us (even those who have been Christians for many years), the eyes of our hearts remain closed. Our hearts are wounded and calloused from the battle of life, and what we really need is a heart transplant. I was someone who was "ever hearing but never understanding" (Matt 13:14), and I desperately wanted to understand. I didn't want to remain stuck in a place of darkness.

We read in Proverbs 4:7 that understanding is of great value: "The beginning of wisdom is this: Get wisdom. Though it cost all you have, get understanding." Though it cost all you have? Well, that certainly makes it seem pretty important.

I first spent time with this verse while doing a study on wisdom, but somehow the understanding part had escaped me. The verse lost its impact because I still equated knowledge with understanding. The Hebrew word for understanding, *binah,* is a feminine word that connotes insight or intuition. Once I experienced a tangible filling of the Father's love, the eyes of my heart were opened, and I realized the meaning of "understanding." Certain passages of scripture took on a deeper and richer significance. They became alive in a way I had never experienced. I had insight that was entirely new. Passages that previously condemned me became life-giving. Through a revelation of God's love, I understood the Word with my heart and not just my mind.

When I speak of revelation, what I am talking about is a divine disclosure. Think of it like an object on a table that is covered by a cloth. You can't tell what is under the cloth until someone removes it and you see the object clearly. Revelation feels like this. God is removing the cloth so we can see something that has always been there. It is a completely different view. Likewise, when the eyes of the heart are opened, we gain a window into the very heart of God. We see things from his perspective—the kingdom perspective.

If I'm honest, it took me a long time to receive this revelation. I had a lot of junk that God needed to clean out of my heart first. The debris of brokenness had clogged up the springs. My heart was obstructed and hard, and I knew it. The callouses mentioned in Matthew 13 were mine. The heart of stone in Ezekiel 36? Also mine. The people with "darkened understanding" because of "their hardness of heart" in Ephesians 4? They were much too familiar.

But it's not as if I wanted to be this way. After I became a Christian, I truly desired an intimate relationship with Jesus. Desperately, I wanted to experience the peace and joy of knowing him. I wanted to change and cried out for it. I wanted to submit all my fear to him, but something inside me was stuck. After working so hard to focus on God's love, I couldn't figure out why nothing changed. If you feel stuck right now, I want you to know you are not alone. I pray you will be encouraged as I share my journey from fear into freedom.

I understand now that I really needed to experience God's love within my heart, but I discovered this type of heart change takes time. It's a process that often involves rebuilding a house with a faulty foundation. There was no use beating myself up for something I couldn't change. I couldn't muster up more faith on my own strength, or reconstruct my foundation. The process must start with God, and he always does the job better than we can imagine. C. S. Lewis brought wonderful perspective to the process when he wrote, "You thought you were being made into a decent little cottage: but He is building a palace. He intends to come and live in it Himself."[2]

What God ultimately showed me about the parable of the sower is that our hearts are on a journey. While we may seem stuck in a place with thorns, his loving-kindness leads us to a place where our hearts become a fertile field that can be cultivated with love. There is no set timetable for this. Every heart is different. We all have our own wounds, our own areas of fear and doubt, our own secret struggles.

But God knows our hearts better than we do, and only he knows how to break up the hard soil and unclog the springs. It often involves forgiveness—forgiving others, seeking forgiveness, and even forgiving ourselves. It can also mean allowing God to show us places along our spiritual walk where we may have developed false ideas about him—that he is harsh and vengeful, rather than patient and kind. These beliefs can block our ability to receive the fullness of his love. And Jesus wants us to receive that fullness. In fact, he prayed for it.

Look at John 17:26: "I made known to them your name, and I will continue to make it known, that the love with which you have loved me may be in them, and I in them" (ESV). Jesus prayed for you and me. He wanted us to know his Father and receive his love. If Jesus asked for this to happen, there are a couple things we can know with certainty. First, this *is* God's will. Second, if we allow him, he will make it a reality.

Every journey is different—as unique as each individual person. Just think about the biblical accounts of healing. Jesus heals many people, but each encounter is different. Who would have guessed that Jesus would spit on the ground to make mud in order to heal a blind man? (John 9:6) With God, it's best to let him write the story. My journey has looked nothing like my husband's, and I've had to be careful not to compare the two. For my husband, the journey has been something like a roller coaster ride with some dramatic ups and downs. Mine has been more like a steady incline. To look at it from one day to the next, you might not recognize any significant change, but over a longer period of time, the change becomes more obvious.

CƷ

Heart surgery is an appropriate analogy to describe what God wants to do for us. That's how it looked for my husband and also for me. I have heard others describe it similarly. God may need to start by putting in a stent. Or maybe it's time for a bypass. Perhaps he'll go straight for a transplant. Wherever he wants to start, he's the surgeon who knows best.

Let me assure you there is a biblical precedent for this type of invasive heart work. I often think we place so much emphasis on "right" thinking that we fail to see what the Bible says about the condition of the human heart. It's not only a New Testament idea either. Our hearts have been a problem since the beginning. Going all the way back to Deuteronomy, we see God emphasizing the importance of heart circumcision for the Israelites. The English word *circumcise* means "to cut around," while the Hebrew root word לוּמ (*mul*), which is often translated as "circumcise," can similarly translate to "cut off."

Deuteronomy 10:16 says, "Circumcise therefore the foreskin of your heart, and be no longer stubborn" (ESV). Later, in Deuteronomy 30:5, we read, "The Lord your God will circumcise your hearts and the hearts of your descendants, so that you may love him with all your heart and with all your soul, and live." What an incredible promise! He will cut off all that enshrouds our hearts, including scar tissue and the other junk that separates us from him. This procedure makes our hearts soft enough to experience his love. It is the cutting of a new covenant—a covenant of love. But we have to be willing to let the surgeon do the cutting.

Paul also emphasizes the necessity of heart work. In his letter to the Romans, who were at risk of adopting a legalistic faith, he addressed the Jewish practice of circumcision with clarity. "A person is not a Jew who is one only outwardly, nor is circumcision merely outward and physical. No, a person is a Jew who is one inwardly; and circumcision is circumcision of the heart, by the Spirit, not by the written code" (Romans 2:25-29). This message is also for us today. The heart matters, and if we don't let God do the inner work, we can't truly belong to him. He wants us to become part of a new family bound by a covenant of love.

Turning back to the Old Testament, the story of Cain and Abel in Genesis 4 provides an excellent illustration. Both brothers made an offering to the Lord, but it says, "The Lord looked with favor on Abel and his offering, but on Cain and his offering he did not look with favor" (Genesis 4:4-5). The difference was the heart attitude behind the offerings. God sees through outward appearances, and the true condition of Cain's heart was exposed when he responded to God's warning by murdering his brother. But we can be sure that Cain's violence was no surprise to a God who looks upon the heart. Likewise, the condition of our hearts is no mystery to God.

Jeremiah 4:3-4 is another wonderful example of God's concern regarding his people's heart condition:

> *Break up your unplowed ground*
> *and do not sow among thorns.*
> *Circumcise yourselves to the Lord,*
> *circumcise your hearts,*
> *you people of Judah and inhabitants of Jerusalem,*
> *or my wrath will flare up and burn like fire*
> *because of the evil you have done—*
> *burn with no one to quench it.*

Break up your unplowed ground! Although I only noticed the significance of this passage recently, it is exactly what the Lord revealed to me as I grappled with the parable of the sower. A hard heart is of no use to God. He can't cultivate love in soil that doesn't yield. The only solution is to let him cut away the hardened parts. When our hearts are left uncircumcised in a hardened state, we experience God differently because we cannot yield to love. This is a painful condition, but praise be to God that he can change the hardest of hearts.

When our hearts are changed, it opens our eyes. This change of perspective allows us to live differently, with greater freedom and peace. We hear God in new ways and understand his truth as we never have before. He brings new life into everything from scripture to worship.

03

Sometimes we come across a passage of scripture that goes straight to the heart. God gives it to us at just the right time to help us along the journey. For me, this was Psalm 27. I honestly don't remember the exact moment it grabbed hold of me, but God highlighted particular verses, and I knew he was speaking to me. Sometimes it felt as if David's words had come from my own heart. It gave me an anchor when I was tossed about by my fears.

This Psalm is often mentioned as an illustration of David's confidence in God, which it certainly is. However, for me, the comfort came from seeing that a man like David was intimately acquainted with fear. It made me feel less alone, less like a failure. No one could write such words without having experienced the struggle. David, a man after God's own heart, was also profoundly human, and so his writing had much to offer in my struggle.

PSALM 27

The Lord is my light and my salvation—
whom shall I fear?
The Lord is the stronghold of my life—
of whom shall I be afraid?

When the wicked advance against me
to devour me,
it is my enemies and my foes
who will stumble and fall.

Though an army besiege me,
my heart will not fear;
though war break out against me,
even then I will be confident.

One thing I ask from the Lord,
this only do I seek:
that I may dwell in the house of the Lord
all the days of my life,
to gaze on the beauty of the Lord
and to seek him in his temple.

For in the day of trouble
he will keep me safe in his dwelling;
he will hide me in the shelter of his sacred tent
and set me high upon a rock.

Then my head will be exalted
above the enemies who surround me;
at his sacred tent I will sacrifice with shouts of joy;
I will sing and make music to the Lord.

Hear my voice when I call, Lord;
be merciful to me and answer me.
My heart says of you, "Seek his face!"
Your face, Lord, I will seek.

Do not hide your face from me,
do not turn your servant away in anger;

you have been my helper.
Do not reject me or forsake me,
God my Savior.

Though my father and mother forsake me,
the Lord will receive me.

Teach me your way, Lord;
lead me in a straight path
because of my oppressors.

Do not turn me over to the desire of my foes,
for false witnesses rise up against me,
spouting malicious accusations.

I remain confident of this:
I will see the goodness of the Lord
in the land of the living.

Wait for the Lord;
be strong and take heart
and wait for the Lord.

There is so much wisdom in this marvelous text. Since it has touched my heart, I often use it with others when I pray for them. I like to read it out loud as they rest and receive. How different parts speak to each individual heart never ceases to amaze me. For me, God started with the last two verses: "I remain confident of this: I will see the goodness of the Lord in the land of the living. Wait for the Lord; be strong and take heart and wait for the Lord" (Psalm 27:13-14).

When I read this during my deepest despair, I felt God saying, *You can trust me for your healing. I've created you for life, not death. Just keep holding on to me.* And so I did. I clung to the promise of that passage with every fiber of my being. As time went on, he spoke through other parts of that scripture. My desire became not only to seek healing, but to seek him—to experience his sheltering love. Little by little, as I encountered more of this love, I stepped into a place where I could "gaze on the beauty of the Lord." When we "seek him in his temple," we are digging deeper into our own hearts, the place where he dwells. This led me into even greater intimacy with God. I recognized in him a safe place to rest. "For in the day of trouble he will keep me safe in his dwelling." My heart learned that it could trust him and that his love was not only a shelter, but a home. My home is with him and in him, and he is safe.

He also showed me he was with me in the waiting. Even when I knew I still had a long way to go, it was okay to wait. I didn't need to feel guilty that I was still a work in progress. His faithfulness would see me through the battle. When we are brought low, he is the one who lifts us up. When we receive more of his love, it brings patience.

Earlier in my journey, I read Psalm 27 in amazement that David could have so much faith. It didn't seem possible. "Though an army besiege me, my heart will not fear." Those bold words made little sense in the prison where I lived. I felt like an army besieged me every single day, and I was far from making such claims about my heart. But David's heart was tuned differently. His heart was connected to his heavenly Father in a way I didn't yet understand.

Today, I read the first lines differently. And this is not because of something I grasped with my mind or intellect. It is because of something I received in my heart. I read David's words and understand at the core of my being that I truly don't need to be afraid. Something has shifted. My heart knows the Father sees me and loves me. When the depth of that love became real in my heart, I finally understood what David meant. Of course, I still I have my own trials. That's life. But God has given me a solid foundation of his love, and I'm finding more and more that it's a safe place to stand.

Questions for Reflection

1. How would you describe the difference between head knowledge and heart understanding?

2. Do you have areas in your life where you feel you've hardened your heart? Are there times when your heart has felt his tender touch?

3. What scripture passages have challenged you in your walk? Are there certain verses that you long to understand better?

Going Deeper

Ask God to bring a scripture passage to mind that he would like you to explore with new eyes. Invite him to open the eyes of your heart and help you see the passage with heart understanding. **Write what he reveals to you.**

> *The beginning of wisdom is this: Get wisdom.*
> *Though it cost all you have, get understanding.*

> — PROVERBS 4:7

CHAPTER 3

A STORY
OF SURRENDER

"The condition for obtaining God's full blessing is absolute surrender to Him."

— ANDREW MURRAY, ABSOLUTE SURRENDER.

Not long after Bruce found freedom from his allergies, I became pregnant with our first child. I was still working, and the pregnancy was trouble-free. Overjoyed about my husband's miraculous healing, I felt like our lives had been restored. Becoming a mother excited me, and although I had mixed feelings about leaving a job on Capitol Hill that I enjoyed, I believed being a stay-at-home mom was the best choice for our family. The demands of political jobs in Washington can be intense, and I knew remaining in my job would be more draining than fulfilling. Many women don't have a choice when the income is essential, but for our family at that time, it seemed to be the best path.

What I never expected was the battle that would consume me from the moment our daughter was born. If you are a mother, you are undoubtedly familiar with the kind of worries I had at first. You give birth to this tiny, fragile human being, and the next thing you know, you're taking them home from the hospital with no idea what you are doing. Every little snort or sneeze causes a hiccup of fear as you question whether those sounds are normal. You may also silently wonder if you're going to be a complete failure at this whole parenthood thing. For some people, these fears gradually subside as practical experience creates a growing sense of confidence. I wish I could say that had been my experience. Rather, becoming a mother was like someone opening a dam that unleashed a torrent of fears I'd previously kept subdued.

Given my struggle with fear of death, it didn't help that my daughter entered the world with unforeseen complications. Labor had been long (fifty-five-hours long!) and difficult. When my beautiful baby girl finally arrived, I think she was as worn out as I was. She struggled to breathe, among other troubling signs. Before I knew it, the nurses whisked her away to intensive care. I insisted my husband accompany her, and I was left alone.

I will never forget lying alone in that hospital room in a fog of confusion. I picked up the phone to call my parents and let them know they had a granddaughter. Just as I dialed the number, a nurse came into the room and told me to hang up. I did so as she curtly told me I had no business making a phone call when I had such a sick little girl. Panic seized my heart. "Is she going to live?" I asked. She couldn't answer my question. And then I was left alone, just me and my fear. I remember trying to pray, but I couldn't break through the fear. It had a veritable chokehold on me and created a barrier that rendered me unable to feel God's presence.

After many tests, including a spinal tap, they gave us a preliminary diagnosis of sepsis. I couldn't wrap my head around how my newborn came into the world with a life-threatening systemic infection. When they released me from the hospital without our baby, I felt helpless. It seemed as if I was already failing as a mother. Thankfully, our daughter's condition improved, and she only spent a few days in the neonatal intensive care unit. However, when we brought our baby home, I could not extricate myself from the fear something was still wrong with our newborn and that I would fail as a mother.

As many new parents have experienced, we spent the weeks that followed in a sleep-deprived fog. Our daughter wasn't feeding well, so after visiting a lactation consultant, I spent my days in a continual pattern of nursing, pumping, and weighing. She rarely slept over twenty minutes at a time during the day, and she cried all night—still screaming as the sun came up. I honestly don't know how she survived, because I barely did. During this time, people were happy to offer all sorts of advice, but I felt if one more person suggested I "sleep while baby sleeps," I was going to punch them.

To say my mental state was impaired is an understatement. I was a train wreck, and I was ashamed. At my postpartum checkup, my doctor used me as a teaching example for her medical school students. She brought three of them into the exam room to interview me about what it felt like to go weeks without adequate sleep or a proper shower. It was a wonderful opportunity to share with perfect strangers that my mental faculties were similar to an average turnip.

After several months, the sleep situation improved, but my mental state didn't recover as quickly as I'd hoped. My daughter was close to a year old when my husband had to go overseas for a business trip. She wasn't sleeping through the night, but I felt things were manageable. I did my best to schedule outings and come up with other ways to keep myself from going stir-crazy during his absence. Unfortunately, things didn't go as planned.

One afternoon, I picked up a popular parenting advice book. As I sat reading about all the things new parents should be vigilant about, from pesticide-laden food to death-trap cribs, one particular danger wormed its way into my brain and wouldn't let go. *Lead paint.* Our little townhouse was over 150 years old. The windowsills were thick with layers of paint, probably dating back to the pre-Civil War period. Suddenly, a new fear seized my heart. Had opening and closing the windows left our floors covered in a residue of invisible lead? Had those last three months of crawling around on our floor given my daughter brain damage? Clearly, I should have been mopping the floors daily and had already failed as a mother.

Without another thought, I was on the phone to the pediatrician's office asking for a blood test as soon as possible. Having lost all ability to think rationally, I was completely unhinged. Convinced I had irreparably harmed my beautiful baby, my mind went into overdrive, and God felt very far away. The worst part was the inability to escape the tormenting circular thoughts that had taken hold.

That was the beginning of my downward spiral into the realm of Obsessive-Compulsive Disorder.

☙

My church referred me to a Christian counselor to help with my struggle, but when the first two appointments proved discouraging, I quit. I couldn't connect with her personality, and her advice seemed to come from her own place of brokenness and fear. I certainly didn't want more fear than I already had, so I put the whole counseling thing on the back burner and pressed on.

Masking my issues as best I could, I tried to appear both rational and functional. (Naturally, those closest to me could see right through the act.) I carried on normal conversations and did normal mom things, but the fear never left my mind. It lurked on the edges of everything I did. While enjoying a playdate outside our home—"Don't touch that toy! You don't know where it was made." While riding a carousel at the park—"Don't put your hand in your mouth! Those ponies are old." Keeping my daughter safe was *my* responsibility, and I could not trust God with the assignment.

I also knew that being terrified of paint wasn't normal, so shame gripped me. This was no way to live. I knew this was not what God wanted for me or my daughter, but I felt powerless. Why couldn't I control my own thoughts? Why couldn't I get my act together and renew my mind with scripture and prayer? I felt like a failure, and I believed God saw me that way too.

A year later, just after our son was born, I started seeing a new counselor. I clicked with her immediately and found her both sympathetic and helpful. The timing couldn't have been better. With a new baby came the inevitable loss of sleep and the stress of caring for a newborn. I was also parenting a toddler who frequently declared that she'd wanted a bunny instead of a brother.

Contributing to my fear was the fact that we lived in Washington, D. C. at the time, and the 9/11 terror attacks had just occurred. It seemed the entire city was caught in a state of PTSD. With everything going on, it didn't take long for the OCD to rise to the surface in an ugly way. Once again, I became terrified of lead paint in our home (and by now we were living in a newer home). I had the help of a terrific part-time nanny, whom we hired to make sure I could get a little extra sleep. But even with her help, I still mopped the kitchen floor repeatedly throughout the day. One afternoon, I showed up fifteen minutes late for a counseling appointment. When the counselor asked why I was late, I could only shake my head and stutter, "I had to mop the floor." I still remember the look of concern in her eyes as she said, "Oh honey, you need some help."

With her assistance, and a period of time on anti-anxiety medication, I pushed through. She gave me scripture to memorize and proclaim. I carried verses with me on notecards and taped them to my mirror and refrigerator. During panic, it helped, but I believe it pushed the problem below the surface.

Eight months later, I encountered another period of significant stress. I had taken my son for his regular checkup. We were due to leave the following day for a much-anticipated lakeside vacation in Vermont, and his checkup was one of many things on my to-do list before leaving. What I'd assumed would be a normal well-child visit turned into a nightmare.

After a brief exam, the pediatrician said she didn't like the sallow color of my son's skin or the look of his growth chart. She left the room only to come back several minutes later and pronounce that my son had stopped growing and she suspected liver failure. She ordered an array of blood tests and explained that she was diagnosing him with failure to thrive. I tried to stay calm as panic fought for control. *Breathe, just breathe.*

I explained we were leaving for vacation and asked if there

was really cause for concern. She looked me straight in the eye and said, "Mrs. Mason, there is *serious* cause for concern." She then told me we could go to Vermont, but we were to feed our son only high-fat, high-calorie foods. If he didn't gain weight in a week to ten days, he would need a feeding tube. She asked for my mobile number and said she would call with the lab results. Various words from her mouth hit me like daggers. *Metabolic disorder. Impaired development. Transplant list.* I felt like I was going to vomit.

We headed to Vermont with a heaviness I had never known. My mind, body, and spirit ached for my little boy. How was this happening? I tried to enjoy lying in a hammock on the shore of Lake Champlain, but relaxation was impossible. Every moment, I feared the dreaded call would come. Six days later, when she called, I was already a wreck. To my surprise, the report was not nearly as serious as we expected. Some of his liver enzymes were abnormal, but not enough to cause great concern. He was to continue his diet of avocado, brie, and Häagen-Dazs ice cream until his next weight check.

This was an immense relief. But I believe the stress and anxiety I encountered that week brought my mind and body to a breaking point. I began experiencing distressing symptoms. Strange bruises developed on both of my forearms, and there was a disconcerting tingling in my hands. My legs felt heavy and clumsy. I dropped things, and sometimes I would wake at night unable to lift my eyelids, as if the muscles were too weak to open them.

I consulted various doctors, but no one had a straightforward answer. They would utter things like carpal tunnel, autoimmune disease, thoracic outlet syndrome, possible MS, and fibromyalgia. I received steroid shots, took anti-inflammatory drugs and an assortment of vitamins, and began physical therapy. Nothing helped. I was miserable and terrified. Not having a solid diagnosis caused my mind to wander toward every worst-case scenario. I convinced myself I was dying.

What started as occasional episodes of panic became an all-encompassing darkness. My thoughts were entirely beyond my control. I tried so hard to fight the battle with every resource suggested to me, but I couldn't seem to step into the light. Every single moment was filled with the fear of death. At first, it had been fear for my children, but the fear was compounded by my health problems. I convinced myself every doctor visit, every phone call, every lab report, would confirm my worst fears.

I remember lying on the dining room floor of our home in Oxford, England, one morning a full three years after the mysterious illness began. I had taken the kids to school, come home and attempted to have quiet time with my Bible and a cup of tea. As I sat at the kitchen table and prayed, a desperation came over me. Physically, I was in pain. Emotionally, I was exhausted. Spiritually, I was stuck. I couldn't do it anymore. I needed a breakthrough. I needed to know God heard my desperate cries and that he could see me.

My husband had a small, smooth cross made of wood. It was carved to fit easily in the hand and used as a focal point of prayer. He had left it on the kitchen table, and I reached for it, tears pouring down my face. Rubbing my thumb over its glossy surface, I walked into the dining room. Suddenly, I stopped at the end of the dining room table, dropped to the green carpeted floor and sobbed. I lay there for some time just crying out to Jesus.

When I opened my eyes, I looked toward our patio door. What I saw captured my attention immediately. Golden sunlight streamed through the trees on the edge of the garden, but one particular beam illuminated a thick green vine growing over the garden wall. In that moment, I heard God's reminder that he is the vine. As my thoughts reoriented to this truth, a warmth came over me, and I knew he heard my cries. He saw my despair. He was with me.

There's a reason Jesus tells us in John 15 that he is the "true vine" and we are to "abide in him." We must be connected to him if we are to thrive. He wants us to receive all that he has—all that the Father has for us. He desires for us to flourish, not wither away under the burden of fear. He says, "As the Father has loved me, so have I loved you. Abide in my love" (John 15:9). When we abide in him, he infuses us with his perfect love.

In that love, fear can no longer stand.

From a place of complete surrender, I looked at what had once been an ordinary garden vine. It seemed the heavens had opened. The golden light pouring over the wall held a promise. I couldn't heal myself, but I knew who could. I also knew that I could trust him. For the first time in many months, I experienced peace.

Helpless surrender is often the only way forward. It positions us to receive. I wasn't praying mighty prayers from my dining room floor. What poured from my heart was nothing more than the desperate cries of a child wanting comfort. And he did comfort me.

I love the truth nineteenth-century South African pastor Andrew Murray shares about the vine and the branch. He draws five profound conclusions about what he calls the "blessed branch-life." First, "it is a life of absolute dependence." The branch has nothing without the vine. Second, it is a life of "deep restfulness." The more we learn to lean on him and put our hearts and minds at rest, the more he pours his love into us through his Spirit. Third, the life of the connected branch is one of "much fruitfulness." Once we depend upon God and rest in him, he works in and through us to produce good fruit. He's the one doing the work, but we have the blessing of experiencing the fruit. Fourth, "the life of the branch is a life of close communion." This is all about abiding. But don't be mistaken, the work of abiding is a heart job, not a brain job. Paradoxically, it is work done in rest and submission. From this place, we can experience unbroken fellowship with the one who is love. Finally, "the life of the branch is a life of absolute surrender."[1] Just as we are to depend upon the true vine for absolutely everything, we are also to submit all that we have to him. He doesn't want us clinging to anything that is not him, least of all fear.

CЗ

Take some time and read through this beautiful poem by Freda Hanbury. I was not familiar with her until I started reading more of Andrew Murray's work. Murray found deep significance in her words. I also want to share them with you.

ONLY A BRANCH

Tis only a little Branch, a thing so fragile and weak, but that little Branch hath a message true to give, could it only speak.

I'm only a little Branch, I live by a life not mine, for the sap that flows through my tendrils small is the life-blood of the Vine.

No power indeed have I the fruit of myself to bear, but since I'm part of the living Vine, its fruitfulness I share.

Dost thou ask how I abide? How this life I can maintain?—I am bound to the Vine by life's strong band, and I only need remain.

*Where first my life was given, in the spot where I
am set, upborne and upheld as the days go by, by
the stem which bears me yet.*

*I fear not the days to come, I dwell not upon the
past, as moment by moment I draw a life, which
for evermore shall last.*

*I bask in the sun's bright beams, which with
sweetness fills my fruit, yet I own not the clusters
hanging there, for they all come from the root.'*

*A life which is not my own, but another's life in
me: This, this is the message the Branch would
speak, a message to thee and me.*

*Oh, struggle not to "abide," nor labor to "bring
forth fruit", but let Jesus unite thee to Himself, as
the Vine's Branch to the root.*

*So simple, so deep, so strong that union with Him
shall be: His life shall forever replace thine own,
and His love shall flow through thee;*

*For His Spirit's fruit is love, and love shall thy life
become, and for evermore on His heart of love Thy
spirit shall have her home.*

Questions for Reflection

1. When you hear the word "surrender," what images come to mind? Are they positive or negative?

2. How has God met you through an act of surrender? What did you learn from the experience?

3. Think back over your faith journey. When were times you knew you were attached to the Vine (Jesus)? When were times you felt disconnected?

Going Deeper

Take a moment and meditate on John 15:4-5. Ask the Lord for deeper revelation about these verses. **Write or draw what he shows you.**

> *Do not be afraid or discouraged… for the battle is not yours, but God's.*

> — 2 CHRONICLES 20:15

CHAPTER 4

FROM BATTLING
TO ABIDING

*"Take rest; a field that has rested gives a
beautiful crop."*

– OVID

Through his Word, God repeatedly reminds us not to be
afraid. But when we are paralyzed by fear, those words can
feel more like a reprimand than assurance. He tells us he is
always with us, but what if we can't feel his presence? It's easy
to blame ourselves for our fear, or our inability to overcome it.
We know what God promises, but when it seems impossible to
take hold of those promises for ourselves, it's easy to fall into
self-condemnation. *What's wrong with me? Why can't I live like
I believe God's words?*

I love this quote from James Jordan, the founder of New
Zealand-based Fatherheart Ministries: "You cannot win the
battle if the inside of you is fighting against you!" That has

certainly been my experience. We can't expect our minds to renew themselves with "positive thinking" when we're so broken our hearts can't believe the positive affirmation. All of our own efforts to fix ourselves become what Solomon called "a chasing after the wind" (Ecc 1:14). Meaningless, utterly meaningless.

If the battle to renew your mind has felt meaningless, my advice is to ask yourself whether you are secure in the understanding that your heavenly Father loves you. Here, I intentionally use the word *understanding* because this is a heart concern. I am not asking whether you know in your mind God loves you, or whether you can quote scripture to prove that God loves you. If you are tempted to say, "God loves everyone, so he must love me," that's not it either. I'm asking whether there is an unshakable certainty deep in your heart that you are his beloved—that you are worthy of his love, and you belong to him. It is this very love that is the door to freedom.

Are you tired of fighting the battle and feeling like every time you take a step forward, the enemy pushes you two steps back? Then stop fighting. Wave the white flag! Surrender. You may ask, "Isn't that just giving up?" No, beloved. The battle is not ours. What matters is who we surrender to. If you surrender to the enemy, that's an undeniably bad idea. But if you surrender to your heavenly Father, nothing could be more beneficial. In perfect kingdom paradox, surrender becomes a place of strength and victory. I want to be clear about this. You can only win your battle through God's love. Love is the most powerful weapon available, but God is the one who deploys it. You can't conjure up enough love in your own heart to win this battle. It must be received. We are simply vessels for his divine love, and God delights in filling us with his very essence. He says, "Remain in me, and I will remain in you" (John 15:4).

So, what does it mean to remain in him? It means that he is our true home, and we are "rooted and established in his love" (Eph 3:17). It means that we are "safe in his dwelling" (Psalm 27:5) and "no longer orphans" (John 14:18). Our identity and our place as his beloved children are secure. Henri Nouwen describes home as "the center of my being where I can hear the voice that says: 'You are my beloved, on you my favor rests.'" When he hears that voice, he knows that he is "home with God" and has "nothing to fear."[1]

Fear skews our perspective. When fear invades, it is easy to wander away from the voice of the One who calls us beloved and believe we are far from home. The inheritance God has for us looks impossible when viewed through the lens of fear. We question his promises instead of stepping forward in confidence as daughters and sons. We forget our Father has never left us and our home is eternal. From this orphan-like position, the enemy continues to steal our peace and our joy.

We must learn to *be* and *receive,* rather than *do* and *prove.* This is a countercultural way to live. Even the Church can put pressure on us to "do more" when we haven't received our breakthrough. Have you heard sermons telling you to contend for your healing, or to remind God of his promise to you? Think about that for a moment. God doesn't forget his promises. He's not sitting on his throne looking down at you saying, "Once she's begged for this ten more times, then I'll release the blessing." This kind of thinking comes from a distorted view of God and of our place in him. *Contend* means "to struggle, compete, or argue." Does that sound like the way a loving father would require his children to interact with him?

☙

Let's look at some scripture passages. There are many examples of God doing the hard work for his children, but these are a few that have spoken to me. I encourage you to ask God to show you other passages as well.

In Genesis 15, we see Abram struggling to believe that God will fulfill his promises. Earlier, in Genesis 13:15, God tells Abram, "All the land that you see I will give to your offspring forever. I will make your offspring like the dust of the earth, so that if anyone could count the dust, then your offspring could be counted." But Abram doesn't have a biological heir, so none of this makes much sense, and he has questions. *How can God possibly fulfill this promise? How can the impossible become possible?* Ever feel that way? I know I do, and I've learned that God doesn't mind our honest questions.

Amid his struggle, Abram encounters God in a vision: "Do not be afraid, Abram. I am your shield, your very great reward"

(15:1). God reaffirms his promise to Abram and seals it with a covenant. It's interesting that one party is asleep as they make the covenant. After bringing the required sacrifices, Abram literally does nothing. The covenant is completed by God alone. God didn't give Abram a set of conditions or require him to prove his worth. He let Abram sleep. Like Abram, we receive the assurance of inheritance in rest, not striving. He is our shield. He fights our battles.

Similarly, I've been struck by the words of Psalm 68:11-13: "The Lord announces the word, and the women who proclaim it are a mighty throng: Kings and armies flee in haste; the women at home divide the plunder. Even while you sleep among the sheep pens, the wings of my dove are sheathed with silver, its feathers with shining gold." During battle, God goes before us to vanquish our foes. The women in this passage receive the benefit of victory, even from the safety of home. And I love how God's blessing flows to his people even as they sleep. What a beautiful image! For Christians, we win the ultimate victory through Jesus' death and resurrection, and the benefit is available to all who make their home in him— allowing him to be both their sword and shield.

So what about Jacob? We know the story of how he wrestled with God in Genesis 32. He had to contend for his blessing, and it didn't come easily. I've revisited the story of Jacob many times lately. He is an interesting character, and in many ways, I have also wrestled with God. But there are different ways of wrestling. One way is to wrestle internally. This happens when we struggle with difficult circumstances or doubt. We ask God the hard questions and seek revelation.

I've been in this position many times. It's perfectly normal to question things like suffering and injustice. And God is big enough to handle our biggest questions. He doesn't get angry with us when we struggle to understand. Does a loving parent get angry when their small child asks philosophical or spiritual questions? Of course not. The parent delights to impart wisdom. Likewise, God delights to increase our understanding. As we already saw in Proverbs 4:7, he implores us to seek divine wisdom and understanding. He doesn't want us wandering around blind to his surrounding kingdom. He wants to open our eyes.

We may ask deeply personal questions. *Lord, why did my pregnancy end in miscarriage? Why am I still in pain? Why is my marriage falling apart?* Or maybe we have more universal questions. *Lord, why can't you put an end to poverty? Why do natural disasters take innocent lives? Why is there so much hatred and violence in our nation?* Again, when we ask with an honest heart, God doesn't condemn us for lacking faith or insight. I suspect he is happy we trust him enough to open our hearts to him.

Wrestling with big questions is a process that can bring revelation and understanding. Rarely is the answer delivered as an instantaneous lightning bolt. But as we come to know God more intimately, we receive his wisdom. We hold the questions a little more loosely, trusting him more completely. Through this process, Jesus takes us from external dependence upon the law—or merely doing the right thing—to internal heart transformation where we become more like him, obedient in love.

The other type of wrestling is that of an orphan, someone who doesn't know their father. These aren't questions as much as they are demands. *God, remember your promise! I'm demanding my blessing right now! I refuse to go through one more day of this!* Have you prayed these kinds of prayers? I know I have, and it's tiring. These demands come from a place of striving rather than a place of rest. It's an external struggle to get what we want. We're not drawing near to our Father inside his house, but standing outside banging on the doors and windows.

Jacob's struggle resulted in a revelation of God's character and also an affirmation of Jacob's identity and call. From this place of understanding, Jacob received his blessing. Unlike Jacob, however, we have already been given a home in Christ. We belong. We are heirs of the blessing Jacob received. If we know who we are, we don't need to contend for a blessing. Our Father gives freely to his children. Again, when we are positioned in Christ, we should never have to struggle with God to receive what is ours. All that he has belongs to us. We may struggle with other spiritual forces; even then, God goes before us. He fights the battle for his children. The burden never falls on us. But we have to let God and his army of angels do the fighting.

Not long after spending time in the story of Jacob, I opened my Bible to Isaiah 44. It wasn't what I had been planning to read that morning, but a previously underlined section stood out:

> *But now listen, Jacob, my servant,*
> *Israel, whom I have chosen.*
> *This is what the Lord says—*
> *he who made you, who formed you in the womb,*
> *and who will help you:*
> *Do not be afraid, Jacob, my servant,*
> *Jeshurun, whom I have chosen.*
> *For I will pour water on the thirsty land,*
> *and streams on the dry ground;*
> *I will pour out my Spirit on your offspring,*
> *and my blessing on your descendants.*
> *They will spring up like grass in a meadow,*
> *like poplar trees by flowing streams.*
> *Some will say, 'I belong to the Lord';*
> *others will call themselves by the name of Jacob;*
> *still others will write on their hand, 'The Lord's,'*
> *and will take the name Israel.*
>
> – ISAIAH 44:1-5

Look closely at these words: "I will pour out my Spirit on your offspring, and my blessing on your descendants." Who are Jacob's offspring? That's you and me. As descendants of Jacob who are in Christ, we have received the outpouring of the Holy Spirit. Our Father's blessing is already ours. We don't have to beg for it. We don't have to remind God of his promise. Do we really think he will forget?

Don't misunderstand. I am not downplaying struggle. If you are reading this book, you have undoubtedly encountered struggles in your life. They can refine and strengthen us, but there is a time to let go. There's a time to acknowledge we only find our victory in Christ. When we try to win the battle on our own strength, we will fail. God always knew this. That's why he created a better way—a way that allows us to experience him and gain all that is his.

I think this bears repeating: we don't have to contend for what is already ours. But we have to be positioned to receive it. Position yourself like a poplar tree next to life-giving, flowing streams. Allow yourself to be planted in *his* meadow. Does he not "clothe the grass of the field?" (Matt 6:30). These are passive positions, images of abiding. When we abide, he clothes us with his love. He fills us with his Spirit and marks us as his own. So stop banging on the windows and sit. Rest at the foot of the one who loves you, who delights to give his children good gifts (Matt 7:11). Let me put it another way: don't miss out on your inheritance by fighting for the crumbs under the table. Sit down at the banquet table with your Father. Enjoy his company and feast with him.

But what about the parable of the persistent widow in Luke 18:1-8? In this parable, Jesus describes a woman who sought justice and wouldn't take no for an answer. I've seen this parable used as an illustration of never giving up the fight to receive our blessing, to keep pounding on the door and make sure your voice is heard. Indeed, Luke 18:1 states, "Jesus told his disciples a parable to show them that they should always pray and not give up." But I think we sometimes view this from the wrong perspective.

We are told the judge to whom she makes her appeal "neither feared God nor cared about men" (Luke 18:2). This judge bears no resemblance to our heavenly Father, and yet, this is how we often approach God with our petitions. We beg and plead, reminding God that he needs to fix our circumstances. But this is not how a beloved child relates to a generous father. Yes, like Jesus says, we "should always pray and never give up," but our God is not stingy or uncaring. He is our loving Father, and we are *always* welcome to come to him with our requests. How much more should we expect a positive response from him than from an uncharitable judge? The difference between the two is 180 degrees, but we sometimes get them confused.

Satan works hard to prevent us from receiving what the Lord desires to give us. Spiritual warfare is real, and sometimes we need to stand our ground and rebuke the attack. God has given us authority to do so. But often, the biggest barrier to receiving from the Lord is found in our hearts. Many times I didn't need an external breakthrough as much as I needed an internal revelation. Obstacles fall away when we recognize our position in Christ and choose to dwell there. It's a simple lesson that is sometimes challenging to live out: when we abide, we receive. And when we live in the light of our Father's love, darkness flees and fear loses its grip.

A common approach to fear and anxiety within the Church says we can take control of our thought process and force out negative thoughts by replacing them with the positive. Really, this isn't much different from popular self-help strategies with a little Jesus thrown into the mix. Some approach this as battle, others approach it as discipline, but it all involves a lot of *doing*. Now, there's nothing wrong with meditating on scripture. Internalizing God's Word is very beneficial. But don't be fooled by "methods" that suggest God is requiring you to work to achieve freedom and peace. Your Father gives his love generously with no strings attached.

One popular Christian book, which relies heavily on neuroscience, lays out a twenty-one-day plan to detox your brain. It involves taking toxic thoughts captive and reinforcing positive ones. At the end of this cycle, if you still struggle with a particular toxic thought, you can repeat the process or move to another cycle with a different thought. Charts within the book cover the science behind the method and provide a roadmap for rewiring your brain. The author emphasizes you can do seventeen of these detox cycles a year. There is also a fair amount of scriptural encouragement woven throughout the text.

It's all very interesting, but honestly, the mere thought of continuously going through these detox cycles is exhausting to me. If I had encountered this book while in the depths of anxiety and OCD, I would have felt overwhelmed by it and condemned myself for being a failure, or I would have become angry and thrown the book out the window. Although science can help us understand how the mind works, much of this approach places undue pressure and guilt on the person who is struggling. People who are struggling don't need to be saddled with more things to do. I don't believe God is waiting for me to figure out a formula, master a set of principles, or understand the science behind my mental health issues before he will step in and rescue me. So where is freedom found? I promise you there is a better way.

೮೩

Freedom starts with rest. Rest is the very place where we are most in tune with God's heart. In Matthew 11:27, Jesus tells us, "No one knows the Father except the Son and those to whom the Son chooses to reveal him." In the very next verse he says, "Come to me, all you who are weary and burdened, and I will give you rest." Jesus came to lead us to the Father. His heart is a place of rest—the place we can be filled to overflowing, the place where we become who he always intended us to be.

God's love is not something we can earn or achieve. If love is the remedy for fear, then no amount of work is ever going to get you closer to freedom. Striving will get you nowhere. The key aspect is the fundamental need to experience what is already yours. The moment you became a Christian, all that belonged to Jesus became yours. Yet you may not experience the fullness of these gifts because you didn't know they are your rightful inheritance. Perhaps you didn't think you could be worthy to receive your Father's unconditional love. Maybe you've spent your life trying to prove you measure up, but you've worn yourself out. Perhaps your heart is hardened by battle scars. It's not a coincidence that Hebrews 4:9, which talks about entering God's rest, includes an important reminder about the state of our hearts. "Today, if you hear his voice, do not harden your hearts."

I urge you to stop and listen for that still small voice. It is the voice of love. He is calling to you. Let him lead you into his loving presence where darkness cannot stand. Let him touch your wounds and fight your battle. Andrew Murray wrote, "Be not afraid, but come just as you are, and even in the midst of your trembling the power of the Holy Spirit will work."[2]

I cannot emphasize this enough; you do not gain access to his arsenal by doing. You gain it by being—by simply being his child and abiding in his love. It is only by aligning yourself with his heart that yours is softened. Resting in your identity as God's beloved and receiving the love he has for you is enough. It is more powerful than any other weapon the world has ever known. So don't be afraid to let go and fall into Love's arms. He's got you and has already won the victory! "As the Father has loved me, so have I loved you. Now remain in my love" (John 15:9).

Questions for Reflection

1. Describe an area of your life where you wrestle with big questions? What has God been teaching you through the struggle?

2. Which of the biblical figures in this chapter do you most identify with? Abram? Jacob? The persistent widow? How might God want to shift your perspective?

3. How would you describe your experience of abiding? Has it been more about doing or being?

Going Deeper

Think of a time when fear took control of how you responded to circumstances. Ask God to show you where he was working during your despair. **Journal what he reveals.**

> *Come to me, all you who are weary and burdened, and I will give you rest. Take my yoke upon you and learn from me, for I am gentle and humble in heart, and you will find rest for your souls. For my yoke is easy and my burden is light.*
>
> *– MATTHEW 11:28-30*

CHAPTER 5

BIG FEARS,
LITTLE FEARS

*"In the midst of every situation where there is no way
out, where nothing is clear, where it is our fault, we
know that there is hope."*

— DIETRICH BONHOEFFER

Your fears may not be the same as mine. Maybe fear of death
isn't the thing that keeps you up at night. But what about fear
of failure? Fear of rejection, abandonment, or loneliness? Fear
of financial insecurity? Fear of not being good enough or smart
enough? Or fear of just not being enough? Any of those ring
a bell? If we're honest, most of us have a laundry list of fears.
Some control us more than others, but they are all capable of
stealing our freedom. A myriad of little day-to-day worries can
drain us of peace just as much as larger existential fears. Small
or large, our fears can prevent us from living the abundant life
God desires for us. They can rob us of kingdom perspective.

One thing I've learned in the healing ministry is that many of our fears are connected to particular moments when we experienced shame. I never learned to deal with the subject of death in a healthy way because the four-year-old me felt she had something to hide. She was ashamed. When we experience shame, fear can take root because we don't want anyone to know about our shame. Shame says, *you screwed up... you're stupid... you're worthless,* so we keep it hidden in the dark. Often, we use control to keep these things hidden and avoid what we believe will be unwanted consequences for our shame being exposed. When control creeps in, it's usually not a conscious decision. You may not even make a connection between your feelings or actions and a particular shameful event.

A friend of mine experienced shame as a young girl while attending a Christian camp. She'd asked for a root beer, never having tried it before, and discovered it was too sweet for her taste. She simply couldn't finish it. A camp leader was angry that she couldn't finish the can and spanked her for being wasteful. She carried that shame into her adult life and developed a habit of finishing *every* drink that is set in front of her—other people's drinks too. It may seem like a small thing—one that an adult may even write off as laughable or no big deal—but it's easy to see shame, fear, and control in operation. Even in the small things, God doesn't want us in bondage to fear.

A small event caused shame, fear, and control to show

up in my husband's life several years ago. Shortly after our daughter was born, friends volunteered to babysit so we could go out for a date night. We were so sleep-deprived we probably shouldn't have been trusted to leave the house. Somehow, we made ourselves look presentable and went to a French bistro near our home. We had a delicious meal, paid the bill, and headed to the door. Suddenly, the *maître d'* appeared and asked my husband what had been wrong with the meal. Confused, he responded everything had been wonderful. It was now the *maître d'*s turn to look confused. It turned out my husband had unintentionally left an embarrassingly low tip. The simple mistake of a sleep-deprived new father embedded itself into my husband's heart as shame. For years since, he has struggled with leaving tips. He doesn't trust his own calculation anymore and always checks the total multiple times. Again, a minor incident resulted in a long-term behavior change.

Certainly, there are many sources of shame more significant than leaving a bad tip. Maybe you're thinking, *This doesn't apply to me. God could never remove the shame from my abortion... my porn addiction... my (fill in the blank).* And this is just the lie the enemy wants you to believe. The beautiful thing is redemption is always available. No matter the source of our shame, God doesn't want us chained to it. God will never tell you you're stupid or worthless because he never sees you that way. Shame doesn't belong in his kingdom. Without healing, shame always bears bad fruit, some of which is fear and control. When we bring our shame before our heavenly Father, his love never fails to change our perspective.

It's useful to look at Genesis 3 to help understand how shame, fear, and control are related and have been with us since the beginning of humanity. Most of us are probably familiar with the story of Adam and Eve. God tells them not to eat from one particular tree in the middle of the garden. Eve is deceived by the crafty serpent, takes some fruit from the forbidden tree, and gives some to her husband. They both eat. But take a close look at the sequence of events here:

> *When the woman saw that the fruit of the tree was good for food and pleasing to the eye, and also desirable for gaining wisdom, she took some and ate it. She also gave some to her husband, who was with her, and he ate it. Then the eyes of both of them were opened, and they realized they were naked; so they sewed fig leaves together and made coverings for themselves.*

> *Then the man and his wife heard the sound of the Lord God as he was walking in the garden in the cool of the day, and they hid from the Lord God among the trees of the garden. But the Lord God called to the man, "Where are you?"*

> *He answered, "I heard you in the garden, and I was afraid because I was naked; so I hid."*

And he said, "Who told you that you were naked?
Have you eaten from the tree that I commanded
you not to eat from?"

— GENESIS 3:6-11

In that moment, shame, fear, and control entered the human story. Adam and Eve realized their mistake immediately as they noticed their nakedness. This feeling of shame was unfamiliar to this couple whose only experience consisted of God's perfect love and acceptance. Suddenly, they knew something was wrong and feared the consequences. So what did they do next? Covering their nakedness with fig leaves, they tried to fix the problem themselves. They tried to take control of the situation rather than turning back to God.

Have you ever experienced that yourself? Have you felt the sting of shame, worried about the outcome, and tried to make things right through your own initiative? It can be an exhausting cycle in which we run round and round without finding any peace. Why? Because we weren't made to live with shame. We were made to experience God's approval, to know that we are safe with him, and to trust that he is the one in control. When these truths are absent from our hearts, we don't feel the freedom to rest and receive. We try to fight fear on our own strength, and we put pressure on ourselves to fix the things that are broken. But the job is never done. There's no rest for the weary, right? My prayer for you is that you experience what David describes in Psalm 68:9: "You gave abundant showers, O God; you refreshed your weary inheritance." Take a moment and let him shower you with his goodness. Let him cleanse you of the weight of shame.

♋

Shame isn't the only thing that needs to be brought before God. Maybe you are one of those people who waits for the other shoe to drop. You believe something bad is just around the corner, even when things are going well. I lived that way for a long time. I don't recommend it. It's a miserable place to spend your life. It robs you of kingdom abundance every single time.

While dealing with chronic illness, if I had a good day or experienced a wonderful moment of joy, I would almost immediately think, *Well, that won't last.* And so it didn't. Once those thoughts crept in, my joy had already been stolen. I could quote scriptural affirmation to myself all day long, but it never broke that thought pattern. So what was wrong? Why couldn't I believe God wanted good and not evil for me?

What I came to realize is that some part of me believed I didn't deserve to be happy and whole. I'm just a sinner, right? Wrong! Even while trapped in my sin, I still mattered to God. He loved me enough to provide a way out. As 2 Corinthians 5:17 tells me, *I'm a new creation.* But I really didn't believe it. My heart had not yet received a revelation of God's love for me as a precious daughter. It wasn't just Jesus' love and acceptance in which I could find assurance. It was also the love and acceptance of his Father—*my* Father.

I can now see that my chronic illness was a source of shame. It shouldn't have been, but it was. At times, well-meaning Christians unwittingly placed that burden on me. Statements like, "You just need to claim your healing!" would leave me undone. It's not like I didn't want to be healed. I cried out for healing constantly. But I felt like I was hanging on to the cross by a sliver, in constant danger of losing my faith. The harder I tried to cling, the more I felt guilty that nothing appeared to improve. Adding to my distress was the thought I didn't deserve to be healed. A relatively pain-free day would throw me into a state of despair over the inevitable return of pain. I felt incapable of experiencing any lasting joy or peace. Part of me believed God judged me for my weak faith, so some sort of punishment waited for me around the next bend.

It took time for God to untangle that jumbled mess of lies, and I had to be gentle with myself as he went about the work I couldn't do on my own. But slowly, things began to change. As it turns out, I didn't need to be afraid of losing my grip on the sliver to which I clung. When we lose our grip, we end up right where we're supposed to be—in the arms of the Father. When we come to the end of our strength, that's where he meets us. When we relinquish control, we find freedom.

As I received the love of the Father, I also understood 1 John 4:18 in a new light. I would often repeat to myself, "perfect love casts out fear," but ignore the next part of the verse, "because fear has to do with punishment. The one who fears is not made perfect in love." I suppose I ignored that last part because I didn't really understand it. In my mind, I knew God wasn't trying to punish me, but my heart held a different belief. My wounded heart had a difficult time receiving good gifts from the Father because I felt unworthy. While I could do battle with my mind and tell myself I was loved, my heart wasn't buying it. I was living in fear because, deep down, my heart believed I deserved punishment.

Now it's not as though I looked for ways to punish myself. Like most people, I wanted to get through each day with a minimal amount of trouble, hassle, or pain. But my heart and my mind weren't in sync. Parts of my heart were mired in disappointment and trauma in places only my Father could reach. Only God's love would bring healing to those areas of my heart.

For many of us, the struggle to believe God truly loves us and wants the best for us is acutely real. In *The Return of the Prodigal Son,* Henri Nouwen words this well. As he encountered increasing measures of God's love and acceptance, his flawed thinking rose to the surface:

> *"Somehow, God's love for me was limited by my*
> *fear of God's power… I have seen how the fear of*
> *becoming subject to God's revenge and punishment*
> *has paralyzed the mental and emotional lives of*

*many people... This paralyzing fear of God is one
of the great human tragedies."[1]*

And yet, how many of us continue to wrestle with this? We
think we're too broken, too sinful, or too weak. We wait for
God to drop the wrathful other shoe on our pitiful selves. But
God doesn't reject his children. Ever. This is why Jesus shares
the parable of the prodigal son. He understands the battles
that occur in and between the human mind and heart, and
he wants us to be free—free from guilt, condemnation, rejection, and shame. The Father waits with open arms, not with
punishment, but with blessing. He wants to welcome us home.

CS

So, what is it that causes you fear? Ask yourself that question,
then ask your Father. The answers may be different. Often,
things we think are our biggest fears may be symptoms of a
more deeply rooted fear. Confronting fear can sometimes feel
like peeling an onion—remove one layer and expose another
below. This peeling process takes time, and the timeline is
different for everyone. Fear of failure was the outer layer of my
onion for a long time. But when my Father took me deeper, he
showed me that fear of failure stemmed from a perceived need
to achieve in order to be noticed. I can now pinpoint several
instances in my childhood when I didn't feel seen or heard.

I remember being forced to play in a basement at a babysit-
ter's house when I was about four years old. I didn't know the

other children, and I found the atmosphere of the unfinished basement frightening. When the door opened and I asked to come up, I was repeatedly told to go back down and play. I was scared, but no one listened. I even got my foot stuck in the sump pump hole, but no one came to help. A root of fear buried itself in my heart. *What about me? Would I ever be heard?*

So what does a child do when he or she feels ignored? They do things to get attention. Some children act out with troublesome behavior. Others become the class clown. Perfection became my vehicle for getting noticed. When your heart decides being perfect is the way to get the affirmation it desires, it must avoid failure. I wasn't satisfied with being a good student; I had to be the best. If there was a solo part at the spring concert, it needed to be mine. If there was a school play, I had to have the lead role. (Incidentally, being given the role of a goat in the first grade play felt like a colossal failure.) Athletics was the only exception. I really didn't care about success on the sports field, probably because I recognized early that speed and coordination were not my areas of strength, so I focused elsewhere. But in the areas where I pushed myself to succeed, the drive was all mine. I don't remember my parents ever putting that pressure on me. It came from somewhere deep within—from the heart of a child who just wanted to know that she mattered, that she was seen.

Much of my early anxiety directly resulted from my fear of failure. And let me tell you, fear of failure can produce some ugly self-centered behavior. If you believe you *must* succeed, how do you respond when you don't? Or when someone else wins the award you desired? In my case, I could easily develop bitterness toward anyone whose success appeared greater than my own. I also experienced a deep sense of shame if my efforts didn't draw high praise from those around me or attain the high standards I'd set for myself.

During my high school years, the sense of entitlement I carried could not have been pleasant for those around me. When we are driven only by our own ambition, we have little room to care about others. The world said it was just my "Type A" competitive personality, or simply who I was, but God showed me otherwise. The more I experienced God's love and acceptance, the less I needed to be first or seek the approval of others. When that old competitive nature rises in me, I recognize the unhealthy desire. It doesn't really fit anymore, and I have no desire to cling to it.

When love enters the picture, we can delight in the success of others and celebrate their achievements. A Christ-centered kingdom focus allows love to flow outward. Jealousy, envy, and bitterness lose their power when our hearts find rest in their true home.

Questions for Reflection

1. What are sources of shame in your life? How do you think shame affects your relationship with God?

2. In what areas of your life do you seek the approval of others over the love of God?

3. Are joy and peace a normal part of your life, or is your experience of them fleeting? If they are not normal for you, what do you think steals your joy and peace?

Going Deeper

Sit quietly for a few moments and ask the Father to give you a word to describe how *he* sees you. What did he say? How does this make you feel? **Write it down. (It's okay if it's a picture or a feeling instead of a word.)**

> *It is for freedom that Christ has set us free. Stand firm, then, and do not let yourselves be burdened again by a yoke of slavery.*
>
> — GALATIANS 5:1

CHAPTER 6

THE MOST EXCELLENT WAY

"Let the root of love be in you: nothing can spring from it but good."

— AUGUSTINE OF HIPPO,
HOMILIES ON THE FIRST EPISTLE OF JOHN

If you've attended many weddings in your life, then you've probably heard the classic "love is patient, love is kind" scripture from 1 Corinthians 13. We often think of this as *the* wedding passage; words that are great for a husband and wife to keep in mind as they begin their life together. But we're selling the apostle Paul's words short if we don't realize his words actually apply to every aspect of our lives, not just marriage. At the end of 1 Corinthians 12, Paul begins the central teaching of his letter by telling the church in Corinth he will show them "the most excellent way"—the way of love. I used to read through this passage and think of it as a lovely sentiment, a good way to live; I didn't dwell too deeply on it until recently. I wish I had better understood "the most excellent way" of love at the beginning of my marriage and in the challenging years that followed.

When my husband and I married, we were both needy people. We were young and broken. We loved each other as best we could, but looking back now, I see the selfishness with which I entered marriage. My husband says the same about himself. Like every human, we each wanted to be loved. And we both mistakenly believed we could draw what we needed from the other. Today, when we lead premarital counseling, we warn couples that this is an unhealthy recipe. We can never expect another person to heal our hearts. A healed heart can only come from God.

Our marriage faced many challenges in the first few years. My husband's health declined drastically not long after our wedding, and his day-to-day needs were challenging for both of us. Learning how to cook for his special dietary requirements, explaining to my coworkers why my husband couldn't attend social events, and making our home a chemical-free environment caused stress in our marriage. At times, I felt my husband was asking more from me than I could give. My heart hadn't encountered enough of God's love to pour freely into my husband. Attempting to draw from a dry well strained us both. But God met my husband in his brokenness during that time, and he discovered the true source of love. I didn't really understand the transition I was witnessing, but I knew my husband was becoming a different person.

A few years later, the tables turned as I struggled with chronic illness. I made demands on my husband that only God could meet. I wanted assurance I was worth loving and wasn't failing as a mother. I needed to know healing was possible. My husband repeatedly spoke love and affirmation over me, and for that I am grateful, but my heart needed to receive those things from God. No matter how much love my husband offered, only God could do the deep heart work required for healing. As God has accomplished much in my heart over the years, I realize the more I receive of his love, the more I am able to love others—including my husband.

1 Corinthians 13 gives us a beautiful picture of who God is. Rather than a list of dos and don'ts, Paul gives us a description of God's character, the very substance of his being that he longs to pour into us. But we have to allow space for him to enter. Because God has given us free will, we must give him access to our hearts. He simply won't do the work without our permission. Shoving in where he is unwanted isn't his style. He's not rude; he's patient and kind. Heart transformation begins when we intentionally invite the One who is love into our inner being and allow him full access.

I love what author and podcaster Emily P. Freeman says:

God is I am. He doesn't just show up. He is.
Silence and stillness are of great value, but only
to the degree that I bring them with me as I enter

*into relationship. Empty rooms by themselves don't
give me much opportunity to love.*[1]

It is important to position ourselves in such a way that
we can meditate on the object of our affection. And from
that position, we receive all the lover has to give: himself.
When we connect to him in intimacy, we are nourished and
sustained. Not only that, we become like him, taking on his
character. We read in 1 John 2:6, "Whoever says he abides
in him ought to walk in the same way in which he walked"
(ESV)—that is to say that we ought to walk in love. We do
not achieve this through our own external effort, but through
internal transformation.

Have you ever known someone who exudes God's love? The
people I have known like this have one thing in common: a
deep inner relationship with God. He has shaped their character. They have allowed him to refine the substance of their
being with his fiery love. I don't know any who would say there
hasn't been a cost. They have surrendered all that separates
them from God and anything that stands in the way of love.
Their willingness to die to self becomes a beautiful reflection
of Jesus.

Dallas Willard wrote, Jesus "calls us to him to impart
himself to us. He does not call us to do what he did, but to
be as he was, permeated with love. Then the doing of what he
did and said becomes the natural expression of who we are
in him."[2] To me, that's a relief. It lets me ease the pressure I

place on myself to do the right thing and appear to have it all figured out. I don't need to do frenzied things I see everyone around me doing—even if they are "good" things. I only need to take a breath and give myself space to step into love. From the place of love, my thoughts and actions take on an entirely distinct character, becoming more Christlike.

What I cannot give you is a blueprint for this process. I'll confess that I lost faith in so-called "how-to" books a while back. I felt I could never measure up. I couldn't pray long enough or memorize enough scripture. I believed my faith wasn't strong enough, that I didn't love God deeply enough. All of my efforts to grow and change felt futile. Perhaps you know the feeling.

Thankfully, that's not how our loving Father wants us to approach him. He doesn't have a list of standards he expects us to meet. He is not withholding his love because we can't "get it together." He just wants our hearts, and this process is different for everyone. There's no set timetable. It's not a race. How he connects with his children is as unique and diverse as the children themselves. The way he meets me won't look exactly like the way he meets you. My husband's heart journey has resembled a roller coaster ride with many ups and downs, whereas mine has been a slow and steady increase I couldn't even perceive at first.

Other people's encounters can certainly inspire and encourage us. Hearing their testimonies can boost our faith and give us a more robust picture of the ways God interacts with his children. Yet at times, I've had to guard my heart against envy. 1 Corinthians 13:4 reminds us that love "does not envy," and that can be a real challenge when you feel as if you're stuck on the sidelines watching others receive a breakthrough.

Later, in Chapter 11, I'll share ways I have encountered God and ways he interacts with people I know. Maybe some of it will have you saying "Me too!" But if not, there's nothing to worry about. Comparison will get us nowhere on this journey. After all, the apostle Paul's encounter with Jesus didn't look like any other encounter in history. All you need to remember is that you are unique, you are loved, and God is helping you with each step.

℔

Perhaps you remember a viral news story about the brother of murder victim Botham Jean hugging the Dallas police officer who shot his brother. Only authentic love has the courage to stand up moments after your brother's killer has been convicted and request to give her a hug. I couldn't watch the video without crying. He forgave her, said he only wanted "the best" for her, and hoped she would give her life to Christ. Certainly, anger or bitterness would be easy to understand. A celebratory gesture for the conviction would be appropriate. But this? No, this was something different, and it was even taken as an offense by some. This was mercy triumphing over judgment (James 2:13), which is only possible through love.

When we experience the substance of God's love and allow it to fill our hearts, there is an outward flow of grace and mercy. As 1 Corinthians 13:5 tells us, love "is not self-seeking." Our ability to love begins with God. It's really not about us or our best efforts. Scripture informs us, "We love because he first loved us" (1 John 4:19). And so, with the love he places in us, we take a greater interest in the well-being of others. We are free to love without an agenda, seeking nothing in return. This is how Jesus loved. When our hearts are transformed from the inside out, we no longer feel the need to keep score. Bob Goff says, "People who are turning into love give their love away freely without any thought about who gets credit for it. Jesus doesn't need credit, and we shouldn't either."[3]

But genuine love can be viewed with suspicion, or even outwardly mocked, by a world that is unfamiliar with it. Some were angry that Brandt Jean chose words of love over words of justice when speaking to his brother's killer. To many, it made little sense. But Jesus' words of forgiveness on the cross didn't make sense to most either (Luke 23:34). The kingdom of love rarely makes sense in a fallen world. An eye for an eye makes a lot more sense. But love? That's radical, even illogical.

Ponder for a moment what our justice system would look like if more people were filled with God's love. The commonplace evils of our broken world would be met with a substance that actually heals. Wounds would be bound instead of being allowed to fester. Light would overtake darkness. Deeds that flow from love would replace actions that rise from fear. We can apply this truth across all segments of human life.

We know from scripture that when love enters, fear flees. "There is no fear in love. But perfect love drives out fear, because fear has to do with punishment. The one who fears is not made perfect in love" (1 John 4:18). In the posture of love, we no longer fear the reaction of our fellow human being or the "what-ifs" of tomorrow. We don't need someone else's approval to feel whole, and we no longer require control over all our circumstances. When we are saturated in this love, there is no place for insecurity or lack. From this firm foundation, we no longer fear rejection because in our hearts we know we are accepted. Take a moment and consider how this might change the way you interact with your church, your neighborhood, your workplace, or your family.

If we're being honest, most of us will probably admit to being not so great at loving others well. Sure, we have our moments. It might be easy to love the sweet lady next door who needs a little help to bring in the garbage cans, but what about that guy who just cut you off in traffic and made an obscene gesture at you? In the heat of the moment, road rage might come more naturally than love. It is human nature. We've all been there.

It's easy to understand when someone who has been hurt experiences anger toward the one who hurt them. But when someone chooses a radically different response to personal pain, the world notices. Why? Because authentic love—the

1 Corinthians 13 kind of love—is precious and rare. The one who truly lives in love no longer takes offense and has no need for revenge. It's right there in 1 Corinthians 13:5: love "is not easily angered. It keeps no record of wrongs." When offense does not come easily, our hearts are free to experience the joy of blessing others.

☙

Lately, I've been thinking about how the Church as a whole would look if more Christians walked in this kind of love. Sadly, in some segments of the Church, love is viewed with skepticism, and anything associated with the heart smacks of dangerous emotionalism. We can easily come to believe that the work of the Holy Spirit is primarily achieved in our minds, as if he wants little to do with our hearts. Following this line of thought, many Christians disengage with their hearts, refusing to recognize shame, trauma, and other heart wounds. This head-heavy—and often judgmental—perspective exists in many Christian traditions. I've fallen into it myself. For many years, I believed that Romans 12:2 had nothing to do with my heart. "Be transformed by the renewing of your mind" felt like a job I had to accomplish with the help of the Holy Spirit, but a job nonetheless. I had an obligation to sort out my thought life and banish my fears. Eventually I came to understand many of the struggles I experienced in my mind originated in my heart. For God to renew my mind, I needed to let him touch my heart wounds.

It devastates me when I encounter faithful Christians who honestly believe God wants them to ignore their pain and soldier on with little more than the power of positive thinking. This approach is exhausting and yields paltry fruit. If there is one thing my journey has taught me, it is this: Christianity that is not connected to the heart is not life-giving. Jesus commanded us to love one another. How is this possible if we allow ourselves to be heart-blind, cutting off God from accessing our hearts? It is impossible to fully love God with only your intellect. It's not an accident the greatest commandment is to "love the Lord your God with all your heart and with all your soul and with all your mind" (Matt 22:37). Love is not one-dimensional and cannot be achieved by the mind alone. Similarly, mere obedience, checking boxes, and following rules isn't love, it's legalism.

Many of our hearts are hard, walled off from the comfort and love God has for us. This is not a surprise to God. He knows why we have built walls, intending to protect ourselves. But he wants our hearts healed, not ignored. As I discussed in Chapter 2, the Bible repeatedly mentions the dangers of a hard heart, and God provides a remedy for his children. Ezekiel 36:26 says, "I will remove from you a heart of stone and give you a heart of flesh." The very next verse contains the promise that he will put his Spirit in us. These two promises are related. The softer our heart is, the more we can experience the life of the Spirit.

My brilliant and big-hearted friend Frank Naea, an anointed

teacher in New Zealand, puts it this way, "You can't have the life of God without the love of God." Think about that. All those things we strive to achieve, the things we think we need to do to become "good Christians"—none of it matters without love. Without love we are an empty shell, lacking the fullness of the substance of God. Authentic love only has one source, and if we wall our hearts off to receiving from the source, we will never live the life God has called us to live. But walls are not the only thing that inhibit our ability to love.

I recently had a quiet morning to read and pray on my patio. We'd been out of town for over a month, and it felt wonderful to be home. Just before we left, we installed a small multi-tiered stone fountain on the patio. I was happy to have the opportunity to observe the fountain again. I enjoy the peaceful sound it makes, and I like watching the water cascade from the four corners of the top level, filling the basin below. This time, as I watched, the fountain became an illustration of the way God pours his love into our hearts, continually filling so that we never become empty.

My little stone fountain is only a few months old, and the basin is solid, but I imagine it could easily develop cracks over time. Extreme cold or even a clumsy accident tipping it onto the bricks below could cause damage. Similarly, a difficult childhood, a broken relationship, grief, poverty, abuse, and countless other things can cause our hearts to become damaged and leaky. If our hearts are no better than a leaky basin, we will eventually run dry. But in God's mercy, we discover the very thing he pours into us also brings healing. The more room we make for his love, the more healing we receive. By allowing God to extract the things that shouldn't be there—like unforgiveness and bitterness—we create heart space. This requires letting go of our own "right" to control things. If I am the one deciding which things need to go, not much is going to change.

Several years ago, I was frustrated and angry at someone with whom I regularly led a Bible study. I think I even described her to my husband as "arrogant and domineering." I complained about her attitude every time I came home, but I couldn't see the problem with my own. My heart was hardened toward her and far out of alignment with God. Later that year, we had an opportunity within our women's ministry to choose a prayer partner. I approached an old friend that I knew would be a comfortable match. To my surprise, my friend said she believed God had someone else for me. I went home and prayed, but the only name that I kept hearing was the "domineering" Bible study teacher. *Seriously, Lord?* I knew I would have to swallow my pride and approach her. It stunned me to hear she had sensed the same thing.

It took time, but as I met with her in prayer and repented of my own critical spirit, my heart softened. It amazed me to see God speaking powerfully during our prayer time, and I knew this would not have happened had I continued to judge her. Eventually, I discovered our hearts were quite similar, and I came to love her. Here, a simple "yes" to what God asked of me resulted in heart healing and abundant blessing.

If I choose to give God full access to my heart, he will lovingly point out pride that lurks in dark corners, envy that simmers just below the surface, and unforgiveness that keeps me in bondage. When God highlights these things in our hearts, he isn't doing it to condemn us. His motivation is always love, and his purpose is to bring healing.

CB

What would happen in your own life if God's love flowed from such an abundant well that there was no room for fear or darkness of any kind? Imagine having your heart so in sync with God's Spirit that the overflow of love utterly transformed your thought life. How would your response to your personal circumstances and the world around you be different? Everything looks different when the eyes of our heart have been opened.

In my own life, I've discovered that more love equals more freedom—freedom to be who God created me to be. This freedom is apparent in many aspects of my life, but especially in freedom from fear. I am more able to take risks without fear of failure. I no longer need someone else's validation to explore new areas of creativity or pursue a new adventure.

As I've already mentioned, fear used to be my constant state. A day (or even a moment) without fear was never the norm, but merely a pleasant deviation from life as usual. Those moments were so rare, I can look back and remember exactly where I was when they happened. I now understand those were instances when God's love broke through. Even then, mired in my own darkness, he was fighting for me, reaching out for my heart.

Psalm 26:3 says, "For your steadfast love is before my eyes, and I walk in your faithfulness" (ESV). Wherever I go, his love goes before me. He is already present in my future, just as he brings healing and redemption to my past shame and sorrow. There is nothing hidden from him. The One who is love stands in the places unknown to us. We need not fear the future when our hearts can trust that God goes before us driving out fear.

Immediately after Psalm 26, we encounter the marvelous first verse of Psalm 27: "The Lord is my light and my salvation, whom shall I fear?" Not only does he go before us, he lights the way. He illuminates the darkness so we can find our way back to him, into his heart, where we experience eternal comfort and security. In his love, we are never alone, never forgotten, never abandoned.

Psalm 63:3 contains another great truth about God's love: "Because your love is better than life, my lips will glorify you." That's a pretty big statement. His love is *better* than life. Think about that for a moment. What does that kind of love actually look like? As I meditated on that verse, I thought of all the things life cannot offer us: safety, security, unlimited joy, and peace. God's love offers all that and more. In God's love, there is no loss, regret, condemnation, or judgment. In short, there is nothing to fear when we are positioned within our Father's love. Even when we experience things that are painful, as naturally happens in life, those things are redeemed by his love. Instead of a damaged, leaky heart, he offers us fullness and contentment. Psalms 63:5 says, "My soul will be satisfied with the richest of foods." Your Father withholds nothing from you. He offers the very best if you will take your place at his table and be filled.

One of the most beautiful aspects of our hearts expanding their capacity to hold love is that we become more like the One who is love. Because he is filling us with his abundance, we increase our ability to impart love as well. We actually become a catalyst for transformation in others. Genuine love isn't static. It is dynamic, flowing, and active. It heals, transforms, and unifies. Once you have received it, you can't help but share it with others.

In his book *Renovated*, neurotheologian Jim Wilder describes the "attachment love" through which we know God and receive his fullness.[4] He emphasizes that this attachment is responsible for the renewing of our minds. Based on my experience, this rings true. Such an image of attachment immediately brings to my mind verses 1-11 of John 15. Being attached to the vine, Jesus, and allowing the gardener, Father, to tend our hearts is the only way we can receive all the love he has for us. Right behavior and good deeds will not get us there. Only God's love brings fullness. This is why Jesus says, "As the Father has loved me, so I have loved you. Now remain in my love" (John 15:9). This is the only way that our "joy may be complete" (John 15:11).

You can't unsee the reality of God's love for you when the eyes of your heart are opened. It pops up everywhere. After receiving a profound revelation of his love during a sabbatical period in New Zealand, I remember being stunned to discover his love in passages of scripture where I had never seen it before. I was given a new lens through which I read scripture. From that moment, nothing was the same. There was a vibrancy I had never encountered. The act of reading God's Word was suddenly full of joyful discovery and no longer felt like duty.

God's love is the single most powerful influence in the universe, and it is contagious. When we receive the divine substance of his love into our being, we carry the light that casts out darkness. This light transforms us and everything around us. "In him was life, and that life was the light of all mankind. The light shines in the darkness, and the darkness has not overcome it" (John 1:4-5). Ask yourself, are you living in that light? Have you allowed his love to penetrate the darkness? Don't underestimate God's desire to make you a vessel for his love. He is always willing.

Questions for Reflection

1. List some words or phrases to describe how you personally experience God's love.

2. Think of a time when God unexpectedly met you with his loving-kindness during a difficult time.

3. Ask God to reveal an area of your life where he would like to bring light into the darkness. Are you willing to let him in?

Going Deeper

Take some time to draw or journal while you meditate on Jesus as the vine and your heavenly Father as the gardener. Ask his love to flow through you as you do this.

*Therefore, be imitators of God, as beloved children.
And walk in love, as Christ loved us and gave himself
up for us, a fragrant offering and sacrifice to God.*

— Ephesians 5:1-2 *(ESV)*

CHAPTER 7

FORGIVENESS
IS ESSENTIAL

*"Forgiveness is the key which unlocks the door of
resentment and the handcuffs of hatred. It breaks
the chains of bitterness and the shackles of selfishness."*

— CORRIE TEN BOOM,
TRAMP FOR THE LORD

For over fifteen years, my husband and I have had the joy
of being involved in healing ministry. In nearly all the prayer
sessions we have led over the years, we found the need to guide
the prayer recipient through prayers of forgiveness. Truly, I
cannot emphasize enough how important forgiveness is in
the process of healing. It is an essential ingredient. For many
people, the biggest barrier to breakthrough is unforgiveness.
Unforgiveness is a deadly poison, and yet we often cling to it
believing it somehow serves a purpose.

I first met Diana at church. She wasn't a regular church

attender, but she would sometimes come to community events. I enjoyed chatting with her and felt a particular warmth for her immediately. At the time, I worked as an aide to our local U.S. Congressman, and one day Diana stopped into the office to see if I could help her with a legal issue. She shared that she had lost her job and pension as a nurse in a big city hospital after being injured on the job. She had sought compensation over the years but encountered one obstacle after another. I told her I would be happy to look into it for her.

Her circumstances moved me and I truly wanted to help, but it became apparent not much could be done. What she hadn't shared was that she had already sought help from every previous member of Congress who had served in our area since the incident occurred over twenty-five years prior. I spent hours combing through her documents, looking for some way forward. I made additional inquiries and discovered necessary steps that had not been taken decades before. After turning over every stone, there was nowhere left to look. It was obvious I couldn't change the outcome.

Throughout this period, Diana shared her physical and emotional challenges with me. She lived with constant pain, and it seemed her body was falling apart. Paranoia took hold of her mental state. She even confided that she heard voices as she worked late into the night to compile documents related to her case. The more she shared, the more bitterness rose to surface. She blamed all her current suffering on the people who had dismissed her from her job and not taken her claim seriously. Her life was consumed by her quest for justice, and her unforgiveness had become a poison that destroyed her physical, mental, and spiritual well-being. An abundance of shame and fear had seized her. The burden of unforgiveness was eating her alive. Her situation was heartbreaking.

One afternoon, I delivered the news to her that our final efforts to find a resolution had been unsuccessful. She was angry at me—at everyone. In that moment, I felt incredible compassion toward her. As she was someone with whom I had prayed in the past, I felt free to speak directly. I took a deep breath and told her I hated to see her carrying this burden. This was destroying her, and it was time to let go. Gently, I told her the only way forward was to try to forgive. Diana looked me in the eye and resolutely declared, "I will *never* forgive the people who did this to me!" Then she stormed out the door.

That was the last time I saw Diana, although she sent a letter sometime later thanking me for my efforts on her behalf. I still think of her with a heavy heart, and I have prayed for her often. Her suffering has been seared into my memory as an illustration of the toxic effects of unforgiveness. This poor woman was so filled with bitterness and resentment, she had no room for love to come with its healing touch. I wept for her, and I believe Jesus did too.

ᘓ

There's a reason Jesus speaks so often about forgiveness. In

Matthew 18:21-22, Peter asks Jesus, "Lord, how many times shall I forgive my brother when he sins against me? Up to seven times?" Jesus responds, "I do not say to you, up to seven times, but up to seventy times seven." What exactly is Jesus saying? Religious leaders in Jesus's day taught that a person was not required to forgive more than three times. To Peter, therefore, I'm sure seven times sounded generous and complete. The number seven is significant because it is often used in scripture to represent completion. But Jesus' response to Peter is quite extraordinary. He challenges Peter's understanding of forgiveness. "Seventy times seven" is a way of saying that there is actually *no limit* to the number of times we should forgive our brother or sister when they wrong us. Jesus is commanding his followers to walk in the higher way of love, a love that is always ready and eager to forgive because love "keeps no record of wrongs" (1 Cor. 13:4). Forgiveness is not a law to obey, but an essential component of abundant life.

If you are like most human beings on the planet, there are probably people in your life you have struggled to forgive. Some of us have had truly horrific things done to us or to the people we love. I always marvel when I read a news story about a parent who has completely forgiven someone who killed their child. I cry every time I hear such a story, because as a parent, I can barely comprehend the amount of supernatural grace that would be necessary for such a thing to occur. Many of us struggle with smaller things. But even in the smaller things, God wants us to be free.

Unforgiveness is an incredible burden to carry. I have seen it spread like a cancer through families from one generation to the next. I've also seen it poison a workplace, damaging everyone's ability to work productively. It is not a stretch to say that it has even devastated nations. Humans have a great capacity to keep a record of wrongs, and the enemy is all too happy to exploit this because he knows its power to destroy.

Conversely, when we embrace forgiveness, it unleashes power for good. Lives are transformed, families restored, and nations are redeemed. Forgiveness is an inseparable component of love, and it is the work of God. While the world clambers for justice, retribution, and revenge, true forgiveness is so countercultural it can be shocking. Walking in forgiveness is kingdom living. It is radically different from what the world expects. In *Surprised by Hope*, N.T. Wright asserts, "Forgiveness is a way of life, God's way of life; God's way *to* life." He uses this analogy to warn against closing our heart to forgiveness. "If you lock up the piano because you don't want to play to somebody, how can God play to you?"[1]

Unforgiveness leads to bitterness, which can only lead to a hardened heart. As I mentioned in the previous chapter, this type of heart receives little of what God wants to give. This is why there's a warning in Hebrews 3:8 not to harden our hearts. When we do so, our hearts become like the rocky places in the parable of the sower, where no seed can grow (Matt 13:5). Jesus is emphatic about forgiveness because he knows unforgiveness hardens our hearts, and he wants our hearts to be soft. If we harbor unforgiveness, we can't receive all the love he has for us.

A few years ago, my husband and I were conducting a healing service at a church in southern Madagascar. A young woman came forward to receive prayer. She wore a head covering and a heavy trench coat. She looked weighed down by her burden and seemed to hide beneath her clothes. She told us she was struggling with some health issues: a headache, generalized aches and pains, and some unusual sores across her chest. She believed her problems were caused by a family member who had gone to the village witch doctor to curse her.

This is not an uncommon scenario in Madagascar, even in their Christian communities. Sometimes, the physical problems presented to us are directly related to the poor (or nonexistent) water supply or something else treatable, like a parasitic infection. But other times there is a supernatural component that must be addressed. In this woman's case, it wouldn't have been appropriate to examine her chest sores in a church service, so we prayed to break any curse she might be under, and for healing and peace. She thanked us and returned to her seat. I watched her as the service continued, bothered that she seemed completely unchanged. She sat hunched over, still wearing her heavy coat. As I prayed for another woman, it suddenly dawned on me. The first woman was carrying a massive burden: unforgiveness.

We asked her to come back to the front. As she knelt before us, we asked if she could forgive the family member whom she believed had cursed her. Her first reaction was that approaching this person would be impossible. We explained she didn't need to go to him directly, that forgiveness is something that takes place in the heart. She suddenly seemed more hopeful and assured us this was something she wanted to do.

As we led her in forgiveness prayer, she literally transformed before our eyes. We could see the weight lifting from her shoulders, and she proclaimed she felt much lighter. After we finished praying with her, she returned to her chair. Within moments, she had removed her coat and scarf and was dancing at the back of the room. I couldn't believe this was the same woman. The change was dramatic. Her chains were gone! The heart transformation that takes place as a result of forgiveness—of self or others—never ceases to amaze me.

You may read this and think, *I can't possibly forgive that person. What they did to me is too horrible. They don't deserve my forgiveness.* Or perhaps, *I can never forgive myself.* These thoughts are certainly understandable, but Jesus doesn't want you weighed down by such burdens. That is why he is so emphatic about the need to forgive. But I don't want to downplay the challenge that forgiveness can be for many people. There are some things that may feel impossible to forgive. If you are a victim of sexual assault, the idea of forgiving your abuser may seem unthinkable.

Throughout my years in healing ministry, I have prayed with many, many women and men who have been the victim of sexual abuse or assault either as children or as adults. The deep and ongoing pain experienced by survivors is substantial and often intense. But there is a very real danger in holding on to unforgiveness towards your abuser. Unforgiveness compels us to relive the hurt repeatedly, keeping us stuck in the pain of our past. It keeps us trapped in continual bondage to the person who hurt us. It opens our hearts to shame and condemnation, fear and doubt, bitterness and hatred. Where unforgiveness remains, we are unable to experience the fullness of healing, freedom, and rest that God has for us.

I've also prayed for many people, not only abuse survivors, who blame and judge themselves for things that are not their fault, such as a loved one's death or their parents' divorce. Others I've prayed for have done something they regret and cannot forgive themselves. Anytime we hold unforgiveness towards ourselves, we construct belief systems, often reinforced by others, that can be a huge barrier to receiving God's love. We might believe we are unworthy of being forgiven. We go to God again and again. We ask for forgiveness but never feel truly free. Perhaps there is a parent or teacher who always made you feel you couldn't measure up, or you could never be good enough. When that belief is written in your heart, it's easy to relate to God out of that wounded place, thinking you don't deserve the love he has for you—including his forgiveness.

I am always surprised by how many people hold unforgiveness toward themselves. Some of the biggest breakthroughs I've witnessed in people's lives have come when an individual forgives themselves. As Henri Nouwen puts it, "One of life's hardest spiritual choices" is whether "to trust or not to trust in God's all-forgiving love."[2] Deciding to trust is powerful, and I have watched people encounter God's love to such an extent they could no longer harbor self-hatred or self-condemnation.

But how do we forgive? Some people teach that forgiveness is just a decision, that you don't need to "feel" anything when you do it. There is something to be said for that, but it is also an oversimplification. At the end of the process, it is the heart that must be set free. Forgiveness is not merely a head-focused action. Deciding to forgive allows God to act in that area of your heart. With any heart healing, God does the work, but we must give him access. Deep wounds take time to heal. It may take time to "feel" differently after we forgive, but that's okay. It is profoundly beautiful when God heals a person's heart to such a degree that they can genuinely experience love and compassion for the person who hurt them. Truly, what could be more Christlike?

When I pray with others regarding unforgiveness, I always approach it as a threefold process. First, we forgive others. This forgiveness may be for a real hurt inflicted upon us or for a perceived hurt that was unintentional. Next, we ask God to forgive us for any unforgiveness, anger, and judgment we have held in our hearts towards the person(s) who hurt us. Finally, if necessary, we forgive ourselves for whatever role we may have played in the hurt being caused. In situations such as sexual abuse, it is the abuser, of course, who is entirely at fault.

But, because of the shame that results from abuse, it is very common for survivors to wrongly place blame on themselves. The survivor may not even realize they have made a judgment against themselves, but the burden of that judgment has caused them significant harm. In such cases, walking through forgiveness of self can be incredibly freeing.

Finally, it is important to remember that God doesn't forgive us because we "deserve it." Forgiveness is an act of grace, not something that can be earned. God forgives because it is his nature to be forgiving. *He is love*, and love keeps no record of wrongs. Similarly, if we want to be love, neither can we keep a record of wrongs. This is exactly what Jesus, the one without sin, demonstrated to us when he declared from the cross, "Father, forgive them, for they do not know what they are doing" (Luke 23:34).

Forgiveness carries such power because it is ultimately an act of love. Love tears down walls and releases the shackles from our heart. It destroys shame, fear, and doubt. Truly, love sets captives free.

Questions for Reflection

1. Are there people in your life you have struggled to forgive?

2. Have you ever experienced the release of forgiveness, either through forgiving someone else or being forgiven? What did that feel like?

3. Do you have areas in your life where you hold unforgiveness toward yourself?

Going Deeper

Picture a person you may need to forgive. Now ask Jesus to show you a person *he* would like you to forgive. Are they the same? Ask Jesus to help you forgive the person he showed you. **Write what you experience.**

> *Love is patient, love is kind. It does not envy, it does not boast, it is not proud. It does not dishonor others, it is not self-seeking, it is not easily angered, it keeps no record of wrongs.*
>
> – I CORINTHIANS 13:4

CHAPTER 8

YOUR TRUE IDENTITY

"Define yourself radically as one beloved by God.
This is the true self. Every other identity is illusion."

— BRENNAN MANNING, ABBA'S CHILD

At the end of Chapter 2, did you ask yourself how God
sees you? What was your answer? Does it reflect the truth of
who you are in Christ—a beloved child of God? Or are you
clinging to feelings of unworthiness and shame? Neurotheologian Dr. Jim Wilder says, "We find our true identities through
a heart that has been given new life in Christ."[1] And this
has everything to do with being attached to the One who is
love. Without this attachment, we can only attempt to exhibit
Christlike characteristics. This is nothing more than "right"
behavior, not true identity, and it places upon the individual
the burden of *should*.

I remember becoming aware of my *shoulds* some years ago as
I sat on my therapist's couch. I always arrived to my appoint-

ments with excuses. I *should* have memorized my scripture verses this week. I *should* have spent more time praying. I *should* have been more patient with my kids. "God's not asking for your shoulds," she told me. It took several years to understand what she meant, but I slowly noticed how many *shoulds* I had in my life.

Sometimes the Christian community can saddle us with guilt or shame when we are told that as Christians, we should have peace and we should experience joy. Of course, peace and joy are fruit of the Spirit. God wants us to live with peace and joy, but when we live from the *shoulds*, it's easy to fall under condemnation. How many sermons have you heard that give you principles for Christian living? How many books have you read with how-to lists for transforming your life? While these things are well-intentioned, they can leave us with a sense of failure or inadequacy. We find ourselves yelling at God, *What's wrong with me? Why can't I get it right?*

We are often led to believe that if we experience an absence of peace or joy, we must not be a "good Christian." In response to this feeling of inadequacy, it is tempting to follow the lead of Adam and Eve by wearing metaphorical fig leaves to cover our sense of failure. Our Christian "fig leaves" can take on many forms and give us a false sense of security. We may become like Mary's sister Martha, who was so busy doing that she could not stop and receive what mattered (Luke 10:38-42). We may strive to assume positions of importance, behaving like the disciples in Luke 22:24 when they argue about which one of them is the greatest. Jesus advises the disciples in Matthew18:4 to become like little children. It makes sense. Children are much more comfortable living without the fig leaves. There is a transparency and self-ease that most young children possess, which is often lost as we grow older and begin to worry about the opinions of others.

Wouldn't it be wonderful to be like King David and dance with abandon before the Lord without caring what anyone else thinks (2 Samuel 6:14-23)? Children do this. I remember watching my four-year-old daughter, without a care in the world, command the dance floor at a wedding. She swayed, twirled, and pranced with unbridled joy, needing no encouragement at all. She was being her true self. But fig leaves cover our true identity and steal our joy.

Fig leaves aren't something we wear solely to look righteous or holy. Worldly fig leaves can be just as harmful to Christians. Do you know anyone whose entire identity is wrapped up in their career? Or perhaps you've encountered people whose fig leaves are an ethnic identity, political affiliation, or social status. Even an illness can become a cover and provide an identity. As I struggled with autoimmune disease, I didn't want to be seen as a "victim" of an ugly disease. Yet the sympathy or attention such a label garners is enticing when you're tired of feeling insignificant or overlooked.

Sadly, when we become comfortable with our own fig leaves, the enemy has us right where he wants us: living from a place of false identity, neither recognizing our position as daughters and sons, nor accepting the depth of the love and grace God has for us. Guilt and shame lurk just behind the fig leaves, but our covering may be so convincing that we even fool ourselves. God wants to address this guilt and shame because we were never meant to carry such burdens, and he knows they weigh us down. God desires for us to live from our true identity, trusting him to be our covering while experiencing freedom and joy.

Here is some good news. You really don't need those fig leaves. God doesn't expect you to be perfect. No one but Jesus has ever lived this human existence perfectly, so give yourself some grace. In your loving Father's eyes, you are not damaged goods. You are the child he adores. He is a good Father. He's there to pick you up when you fall, comfort you when you hurt, encourage you when you struggle, and give you all that belongs to him. He looks upon you with delight—even if you don't believe it yet.

I spent years convinced I was an ugly weed growing from bad soil, but God never saw me that way. He never gave up on me and never left me to sort the mess out myself. He's not a pull-yourself-up-by-your-bootstraps kind of God. He's a "give me your hand (or better yet, your heart) and let me do the heavy lifting" God. But we have to let him do the work, and sometimes it is far too easy to wall ourselves off, declare that we are "fine," and carry on with life as usual. Unfortunately, that approach never leads to healing. Maybe you've already experienced that self-inflicted dead end. Giving God access to our wounds is the only way to see lasting change. The timeline looks different for everyone because we all have unique layers he wants to deal with in our hearts. My wounds, both self-inflected and otherwise, are not the same as yours. But I promise you, God knows just the way to make your heart whole.

It was a personal experience of God's love that finally allowed me to believe that he intended good *for me*. Reading about God's love in scripture is an important practice, but if your heart is walled off to experiencing that love, all you gain is head knowledge. Head knowledge failed to provide the peace I sought, but God gradually softened my heart in order for me to receive what I so deeply desired.

Today, I understand at a much deeper level that his heart was and always will be *for* me, not against me. It has become easier to live from that place of love and acceptance. If there's a part of you that believes your heart is bad soil, or you can identify with feeling like an ugly weed, I promise God wants to reveal your true identity. He wants you to live without the fig leaves. Are you willing to receive his truth, to embrace who he created you to be? Checking all the items off a Christian how-to list will never get you there, but God's love will. Let him help you remove those fig leaves.

ॐ

Have you ever hidden from God? I know it doesn't really

work. It's like a young child playing hide-and-seek who only sticks their head behind a sofa, thinking that the rest of their body can't be seen. I am embarrassed to say I've played that game with God.

It's not an easy story for me to share. Truthfully, I spent over four months of my second pregnancy hiding from God. My husband and I were thrilled when, at twenty weeks, my ultrasound showed we would have a boy. The pregnancy was progressing normally, and there was no cause for concern. Shortly after this, I woke in the middle of the night drenched in sweat with my heart pounding. I'd had a horrific nightmare that our newborn son was plagued with a multitude of serious birth defects. It filled me with panic. I wish I could say I asked God to comfort me and show me the truth about the nightmare, but I didn't.

My struggle with identity and my view of God at that point caused me to retreat from his goodness. I was convinced that God had given me the dream in order to prepare me for the inevitable. On some level, I believed I wasn't a very good mother, so I didn't deserve to have another healthy child. I also didn't believe that God actually loved me, so why would he bless me? I understand now that the root of my panic was a fear of punishment. There is just so much wrong with this thinking, but it's an accurate picture of both my heart and mind at the time.

I'm sure there is someone reading this book with a special

needs child who is an incredible blessing. All children are a blessing, and I believe special needs children have a unique place in God's heart. Please don't misunderstand my story. I am most emphatically *not* saying that children born with disabilities are a punishment. This could not be further from the truth. I honestly didn't believe I was strong enough (or loving enough) to care for a child with special needs. My perception arose from a heart that was wounded and afraid. At the core of my being, I did not understand what it meant to be a child of God. I didn't trust him, because I didn't truly know him. And when we don't know our Father, we can't truly know ourselves. We find our entire identity in him.

Does a good father punish his child by meting out misfortune and despair? Of course not. But I couldn't yet grasp his goodness. His deep love for me wasn't something my heart had internalized, so I didn't understand what it meant to be his beloved daughter. I wasn't living in my true identity, and this played out for some time, causing me to live in shame.

After my nightmare, I became consumed with fear that what I had seen was the truth. Today, I know God as my comforter, so I'd like to think my first reaction would be to turn to him for revelation about a dream and for the comfort only he can give. Back then, my first reaction was to run and hide. I was like the child sticking her head behind the sofa trying to disappear.

So what did I do with my fear? I stopped praying. Seriously.

For the next four months, I literally didn't talk to God, and I didn't listen to him either. Somewhere in my head it made sense that if I shut myself off from God, I wouldn't have to hear anything I didn't want to hear. He wouldn't confirm my worst fears for my child. So there I was, with my precious boy growing inside me, caught in a paralyzing fear cycle and refusing to seek comfort from the One who is comfort. Oy!

Now let me add the real kicker. My son was born in Washington, D. C., in October 2001. Five weeks before my son was born, a large commercial jet crashed into a building near our home and everything in our Beltway bubble turned upside down. September 11 was the day I started having contractions, and the flaming Pentagon building was between our home and the hospital where I planned to deliver. Thankfully, my saint of a doctor met me on the twelfth to help slow the contractions. But my mental state did not improve over the next month as some misguided soul thought it would be a great idea to send anonymous packets of anthrax through the mail. My friends who worked on Capitol Hill were taking powerful antibiotics as a precaution. One hospital in the area had detected anthrax in the ventilation system, and everyone was afraid to touch their mail. The spirit of anxiety was palpable. And there I was, nearly nine months pregnant, stubbornly refusing to pray.

When the day of my son's delivery arrived, I paced up and down the corridors of Georgetown's maternity ward with a tumultuous mix of emotions, while trying to appear like a "normal" expectant mother. And yet, the memory of the nightmare stung at the core of my being. I was ashamed. I felt like I had some horrible, dirty secret. How was I going to love this child that I was afraid to bear?

At long last, I laid eyes upon my son. His big, inquisitive eyes looked up at me from a perfect little round face. The moment was magical and much of my fear ebbed away, but even then, I wanted confirmation. Was there something I wasn't seeing? The beautiful thing is that even though I had spent months avoiding God, he wasn't avoiding me. He saw my fears, and he knew what I needed to hear.

Early the next morning, a pediatrician arrived in my room to assess my newborn son. He held him up and declared, "He's perfect!" My aching heart knew those words were a gift from God. Finally, all my fear rushed away, and I wept, releasing my suppressed emotions as the goodness of God overcame me. Even then, it took time to forgive myself for the stubborn foolishness of not trusting God with my child. I mourned for the months of missed opportunities to pray for him. But God can even redeem time, and I know my child is not lacking anything because of my failure to pray. God is bigger than my failures, and he loves my son even more than I can imagine.

Although my struggle with identity didn't end there, it was a pivotal moment for me. It was then that I recognized God was with me all along, even when I hid. I understood that I *really* had a loving Father who took no delight in my suffering and only waited for me to turn to him.

Our minds can get us into all sorts of trouble, especially when we're not secure in our identity as beloved children of God. I had allowed my mind to run wild with the ridiculous notion that hiding from God was a good idea. Author Maria Furlough says, "In our finite minds, we cannot comprehend the complexities of our futures. We *can* calculate all the what-ifs and the whys, and so we fear. We fear because ultimately we wonder if we can trust God to do his job well."[2] That was certainly my problem. But God met me in that place of fear and showed me his great love, for both me and my son. There had been no reason to fear.

☙

The best way to understand the importance of identity is to look at Jesus. Consider the account of Jesus' baptism in Matthew 3:16-17:

> *As soon as Jesus was baptized, he went up out of the water. At that moment heaven was opened, and he saw the Spirit of God descending like a dove and alighting on him. And a voice from heaven said, "This is my Son, whom I love; with him I am well pleased."*

This is Jesus we're talking about. God himself. And yet, his Father sees fit to confirm Jesus' identity at the moment of baptism. The words spoken from heaven confirm to us that Jesus is indeed the Son of God, but they also confirm in Jesus the truth of his identity as a beloved son. Jesus is empowered by the Holy Spirit in that moment and given authority to act on behalf of his Father. Not only that—and this is my favorite part—Jesus' Father tells him he is loved. Wow! Words of love spoken within the Holy Trinity himself. This is an amazing glimpse into the nature of the Godhead. It's completely mind blowing that we are invited into this very relationship. We—you and me, in all our human weakness—get to share in this incredible love for all of eternity. This is the place from which our identity flows, the very fount of eternal love.

But did you ever consider what happens right after Jesus is baptized? It's not all smooth sailing from that moment forward. Matthew 4 begins, "Then Jesus was led by the Spirit into the desert to be tempted by the devil." Yikes! I know I wouldn't choose that for my baptismal celebration. But this is so important. Jesus doesn't face this temptation from a place of weakness. Sure, he fasted forty days, but when Satan comes to tempt him, Jesus responds from a place of strength. He knows who he is. He is the beloved Son of his Father.

A couple years ago, I had a vivid dream that perfectly illustrates the importance of identity in our journey. In the dream, I walked with two other women on a gloriously sunny day. We were all dressed in pretty pastels, with matching hats and pumps. One woman was the Duchess of Cambridge, Kate Middleton. The other woman was unknown to me, but clearly a close friend of Kate's. We were headed to the palace for a garden party, and I was thrilled to be included. Before reaching the palace, we came to the edge of a large quarry filled with water. Without hesitation, Kate jumped into the water. She effortlessly reached the other side, looking as well-coiffed and put together as she had before the swim. Her friend immediately followed suit. She also stepped out on the other side, as if this whole scenario was no trouble at all.

Then it was my turn. I looked into the water and wondered how I could jump without losing my hat and shoes. As I hesitated, the scene before me changed. I was instantly transported to the far end of the quarry. The bright sunshine faded and everything around me became dim. I knew I would still need to cross the quarry, but it had suddenly become more difficult. The distance across was greater on this end, and the dim light made it hard to see. There were also several other people struggling to get across. Some claimed to be distant members of the Royal Family and others were onlookers. As I walked toward the edge of the quarry, they stripped me of what I was wearing and warned the water would be cold. I knew I would have to jump, but I was fearful. This was so drastically different from the way it would have played out had I simply followed Kate and her friend.

The next morning, I prayed about the dream, and it seemed perfectly clear. Kate knew who she was and where she was going. Her position was secure. Likewise, her well-dressed friend had no doubt she belonged with royalty. She fit the part. I was not so sure I belonged with these beautiful, confident people. What business did I have going to a garden party at the palace? And so I hesitated. I questioned my position. I wondered if I was "doing it right." With that, everything suddenly became harder. Fear and darkness entered the picture. Sure, I was still headed to the same place, but the joy and excitement of the journey had been replaced with apprehension and frustration. But it didn't need to be that way.

When we know who we are—God's beloved sons and daughters—the journey becomes easier, the burden lighter. We have confidence to go where our Father leads because we know we belong. We aren't just tagging along to some royal party. We are royalty. We have authority, and we have the blessing of the Father. His palace is ours.

⚘

As my identity became more grounded in my heavenly Father, I noticed other changes in the way I responded to certain situations. For much of my life, I had been afraid of looking stupid or making a fool of myself. Sometimes I tried to stretch myself by taking risks or stepping outside my comfort zone, but I still lived in fear of being humiliated. Then something strange happened one day in a supermarket aisle.

It was early May, and apparently Cinco de Mayo salsa sales hadn't gone as well as expected. As I pushed my cart around the corner, the wheel clipped the bottom of a cardboard crate. As the crate shifted, I looked up to see a tower of identical crates filled with glass salsa jars teetering from the impact. In a futile attempt to avoid disaster, I lunged forward, and the tower crashed down on me. Salsa covered my jeans and dripped into my open-toed suede booties. A glass-filled sea of red expanded in front of me. I stood for a moment, stunned beyond words. I noticed a supermarket employee take off running the other way. Nobody offered to help.

The old me would probably have left my cart and slunk off to a bathroom stall where I would do my best to wipe off the salsa while sobbing. Humiliation and rage would have consumed me, and I would have waited some time before trying to sneak out of the store unseen. But this was the new me—so different I hardly recognized myself. As I looked down at my salsa covered booties, I couldn't help but laugh. I looked ridiculous, but I didn't care. Were other people laughing at me? Probably, but for the first time in my life it didn't matter. The situation was utterly hilarious, and I continued to find humor in it even as a little boy shouted, "Hey, Grandma! What happened to that lady?" Well, thank heaven for Grandma, who provided me with her wet wipes!

That afternoon in the supermarket was an epiphany. I had truly been changed. I wasn't perfect, and it didn't matter if others knew it. I was free to laugh at myself and the absurdity of the situation. Shame and humiliation had lost their hold on me. I realized who I was—*whose* I was. All that mattered was I was loved, even if I was standing in a supermarket covered in salsa.

Henri Nouwen wrote, "Spiritual identity means we are not what we do or what people say about us. And we are not what we have. We are the beloved daughters and sons of God."[3]

Discovering the reality of our true spiritual identity at a heart level is probably the most liberating thing we can experience. It provides a completely different lens through which to view ourselves and those around us.

1 Corinthians 13:12 helps us understand this better. "For now we see through a glass, darkly; but then face to face: now I know in part; but then shall I know even as also I am known" (KJV). Paul understood that we all suffer from distorted vision. We see through the world's darkened lens and through our own wounds. But the more we step into the light of our God-given identity, the better our vision becomes, and the more we see ourselves and others around us the way God does. It's a process that will not be completed in this lifetime. Yet when we allow God's love to consume us, we come closer to that true vision and knowing our true selves.

Questions for Reflection

1. Are there times when you have hidden from God? Describe the "fig leaves" you have worn.

2. What does the relationship within the Trinity say to you about what God desires in your relationship with him?

3. Have you been tempted to question your own identity and calling? How did you deal with the temptation?

Going Deeper

Take a few moments and ask God to reveal anything you are currently hiding from him. Ask God to show you the "fig leaves" he wants to remove. Ask him what he would like to reveal about your true identity. **Draw or journal what he shows you.**

> *See what great love the Father has lavished on us,*
> *that we should be called children of God! And that*
> *is what we are!*

> – I JOHN 3:I

CHAPTER 9

THE QUALITY OF
ETERNAL LIFE

*"Heaven, once attained, will work backwards and
turn even that agony into a glory."*

– C. S. LEWIS, THE GREAT DIVORCE

After I became a Christian, I spent years wondering why I
didn't have the peace I craved. Why didn't I have any sense
of assurance of eternal life? This couldn't be all Christianity
had to offer. I lived in a near-constant state of fear and doubt.
I judged myself. I pleaded with God like the father of the boy
who receives deliverance in Mark 9, "I do believe; help me
overcome my unbelief." What if I had it all wrong? What if my
entire Christian walk was a lie? What if none of God's promises were true? Or worse, what if his promises were true, but
not for me? Something *was* missing. I just didn't know what.
But when I finally found the missing piece, I knew it was real.

Looking back, I recognize that a part of me knew it was my

heart. While my husband and I were at seminary in the United Kingdom, I put together an off-campus women's retreat. We had worship, a meal and a country walk, a little teaching, and an extended time of soaking prayer with space for journaling and drawing. Feeling the day had gone well, I let myself join in the soaking. I still remember being surprised at the cry that came from my heart that day. It was as if God's words to Ezekiel (36:26) took on life within me. I needed a new heart. I begged God to take my heart of stone and give me a heart of flesh. I left the retreat a little disappointed I hadn't experienced some radical change, but I believe something opened within me that day. While I couldn't recognize it at the time, my heart took on a receiving posture. I experienced a gentle *drip, drip, drip* as God enacted the change I longed for. It was almost imperceptible at first, but eventually I understood I was receiving something new, something *other*. I was receiving the substance of love.

Over the next decade, I gradually moved from a place of fear and doubt to a place of peace and assurance. The process was so slow I didn't realize what was happening for some time. In hindsight, the change is obvious. I am not the same person I was when I walked into that retreat. My heart is softer. I am more able to receive love just as I am more able to love and forgive others. I believe my life has value in God's eyes. While I know I won't achieve perfection on this earth, I am better able to extend grace to myself than I once was.

It didn't all happen at once. I didn't just wake up one

morning so full of love that it was oozing out of me. Although I would receive a more sudden and dramatic revelation some years later, I now see that God was at work well before I was even aware. There were many more impassioned cries for healing and desperate prayers for deliverance, but over time, I saw evidence of my changing heart. The people closest to me, and a few others that I barely knew, noticed as well.

One November, I discovered a lump in my breast. A visit to my doctor, followed by imaging and a visit to a surgeon, resulted in a scheduled lumpectomy. The odds were decent that it was benign, but it was questionable enough that they recommended removal. A few years before, this sort of uncertainty would have left me in a state of panic. Surprisingly, as the doctor gave me his recommendation, I felt complete peace.

This remarkable new peace continued through the coming days. I was so unconcerned that I didn't dwell on the upcoming procedure, and I didn't even think to ask anyone to pray. When I came out of the operating room, I was still at peace. The doctor was amazed when he came in to give me the report. He couldn't believe I was so relaxed. Honestly, I couldn't believe it either. Where was the panicked, hyperventilating me? When he told me he believed the removed lump was harmless, I wasn't surprised. In my heart, I'd known this all along. While I was happy the offending lump was gone, I was even happier to experience what felt like a spiritual heart transplant. Without the circular thoughts and constant anxiety, I was learning to really live.

C3

The fullest revelation of God's love I had yet to receive came during a time of retreat in New Zealand. My husband and I had the opportunity to spend three months on a remote island sixty miles from Auckland. During this time, we lived in community with about sixty other Christians from across the globe. We all came for one reason: to learn to live in the love of the Father. In our hectic twenty-first-century world, much can be said for spending three months off the grid with no access to Starbucks or other modern amenities we often take for granted. My surroundings compelled me to slow down, unplug, and rediscover a healthier rhythm of life.

Each morning we would hear teachings on the Father's heart and what it means to live as daughters and sons of a loving Father. This biblical teaching wasn't of the academic variety, but geared toward heart understanding instead of head knowledge. The afternoons allowed ample time for rest and reflection. They encouraged us to relax and receive. Being surrounded by pristine beaches and majestic mountains along with lush valleys and crystal waterfalls certainly didn't hurt the relaxation process. It was an ideal place to let God do heart surgery.

During our third week, as I recovered from a terrible cold, I lounged on pillows at the back of the room during our teaching time. The ministry's founder, James Jordan, was speaking. I wasn't feeling great and my attention wandered, so I honestly can't recall the content of his teaching that day. What I remember is suddenly feeling that something had physically hit my chest. I don't have any better way to describe it. At that moment, I felt the urge to open a devotional book I had with me. I turned to the page for that day and it spoke to me about finding life in the Father, which reflected James's teaching at that moment. I can't really explain why, but I wept. This may not seem remarkable, but for me this was far from ordinary. Until that moment, I had never been an extremely demonstrative person in worship or otherwise, and I often felt left out when the Spirit was moving and everyone seemed to receive but me. Crying for no particular reason was a huge indicator that God was doing a work in my heart.

For days, I knew something significant had occurred, but I didn't really have language for it. I tried drawing an interpretation of my experience. The image was a fiery arrow penetrating deeply into my heart. During the teaching time about a week later, I received some clarification. Again, I can't recall the greater context of the lesson, but I heard one sentence that took hold of me in a way I'd never experienced: "Eternal life is a quality of life that is from the Father." It was like the lights suddenly switched on. That one sentence made so much sense of my journey. It was the *quality* of eternal life I had been missing. In my mind, I knew I received eternal life when I accepted Jesus at nineteen, but my heart was disconnected from this reality. I had never lived like someone who had found their true home. My heart needed to receive the Father's love in order to experience the assurance and peace I longed for.

And suddenly I knew I had received an impartation of that divine love the week before. My heart had found its home.

The way this transformation occurred was drastically different than following a prescribed method or exercising better self-discipline over my mind. In fact, it didn't look at all like what I had tried for so long. I hadn't wielded the "right" words or rebuked the offending thoughts until they finally vanished. I wasn't *doing* anything when it happened. I had simply positioned myself to receive. At its core, what happened that day had nothing to do with my mind, and yet my mind was a beneficiary of the change.

I can't tell you I haven't experienced fear or anxiety since that moment, but I can tell you it no longer has control over me. What I have experienced is a new level of peace and joy that feels foundational. I used to have fleeting moments of peace or joy that would surface, then disappear. After love filled my heart, joy and peace became the norm. I no longer had to dig deep to find them. Now, when fear and anxiety make an appearance, they are easy to recognize because they don't belong in my new landscape. They no longer seem like insurmountable obstacles. The peace I have received as an elemental part of the Father's love feels like a mighty river instead of the old, barely bubbling spring. It is as if my "normal" got flipped on its head, and I am so grateful for this change of perspective.

03

Over time, as I rested in Father's love, I realized all my feeble attempts to produce the fruit of the Spirit in my own life were pointless. Galatians 5:22-23 tells us, "The fruit of the spirit is love, joy, peace, patience, kindness, goodness, faithfulness, gentleness and self-control." We often try to be more patient or to have more faith, but we have no ability to produce this fruit on our own. Fruit is only generated by the love of God through the Spirit. Knowing the priority of love throughout scripture, I see the fruit of the Spirit consisting entirely of love but containing seeds for each individual attribute. When we receive love, we receive the other attributes as well. So when I received an impartation of the Father's love, I noticed an increase of joy and peace and could trust that he was producing in me the remaining attributes.

How many of us have prayed to have more patience? I know I have. I've even become impatient waiting for God to give me patience. Most often on my journey, I become impatient with myself for not being more healed, more faithful, or further along the path than I am. But I am learning to be more gentle and forgiving toward myself. Deep wounds need time to heal, and the healing often happens from the inside out, so it's hard to see at first. As we walk more and more in God's love, he gives us the patience we lack, just as he cultivates other attributes of his love in our lives.

Even as Christians, it's normal and appropriate to have a feeling that there must be something more. We live in an in-between place with one foot in the kingdom and our other foot stuck (for the moment) in our broken world. Life isn't always easy. Sometimes it can seem downright awful. Bad things happen, even to the faithful. Nowhere in scripture are we promised a problem-free life. But he doesn't leave us to navigate the troubles alone or without comfort.

There are many things that don't make sense this side of heaven. When I look at something like the Rwandan Genocide, there's no way to view that with rose-colored glasses. All I can say is, *Why, God, why?* I can also look at the suffering of friends, family members, or individuals in the community and shake my head in disbelief or confusion. Why did a young mother of four beautiful children lose her battle with cancer? Why did an entire family die in a car accident on the way to the airport for a mission trip? Why are millions trapped in slavery and trafficking? Why do people still die of hunger? Apart from the simple fact that we live in a broken world, there are no good answers. And God doesn't require us to have it all figured out. Our part is much simpler than we often make it out to be.

Let me put it differently: you don't have to have all your theology sorted out or understand everything God is doing. You are not required to know why evil exists in the world. It's fine to ponder the deep questions of existence and ask God for his perspective. Sometimes he gives us divine insight, but our role in the process is simply to surrender and receive. The problem of sin and suffering in the world is not something Jesus wants us to carry. That's his job. That's why he came—and he is more than able to carry the weight. Likewise, he doesn't want us bearing guilt and shame when we don't understand what's happening or can't see the big picture. He simply wants us to come to him for comfort. From that place of comfort, we are better equipped to minister his love to our broken world.

Becoming a Christian doesn't make you immune to tragic events. Jesus said, "I have told you these things, so that in me you may have peace. In this world you will have trouble. But take heart! I have overcome the world" (John 16:33). So what does it mean to have peace? And how can we really attain joy? I would suggest that it means having a different heart perspective—a key component of the quality of eternal life.

In C. S. Lewis' autobiographical book *Surprised by Joy*, he writes about "the inconsolable longing" in the heart for something that seems impossible to articulate.[1] He uses the German word *sehnsucht* as the closest approximation to this feeling.[2] It is what we experience when missing something we can't quite put our finger on. Nostalgia perhaps, but for the future rather than the past. It's the feeling you get when you gaze in awe at a majestic mountain range or ponder the vast expanse of the sea. It resembles wonder, yet is a knowing there is more—a recognition that this imperfect world is not our true home.

When I first read *Surprised by Joy* as a young Christian, this sense of *sehnsucht* was all too familiar. It was a feeling I remembered experiencing even as a child. In a way, it was the fire that kept me searching for more. Years later, when I received an impartation of the Father's love, the pieces fell into place. To be sure, I still experience the sensation of longing. I don't imagine this will end until I have both feet in the kingdom. But now I also experience a remarkable new sensation of contentment. Peace and joy have become more of a constant stream that flows just below the surface, abundant and ever present. They are not abstract concepts that will elude us for as long as we walk on earth. Peace and joy are a tangible part of the quality of eternal life that is available to us now. And yet, so many Christians believe they are required to produce this fruit by their own effort. No wonder we're exhausted.

Many Christians are right where the enemy wants them, allowing themselves to be robbed of the abundance God freely gives. "The thief comes only to steal and kill and destroy; I have come that they may have life, and have it to the full" (John 10:10). But we are often blind to kingdom reality, experiencing a darkness that is not God's will for us.

When the love of God opens the eyes of our hearts, we experience a fundamental change. We view our lives from a different perspective. I love what Andrew Murray says about the importance of the heart: "The Kingdom of God consists entirely in the state of the heart. Therefore, God can ask for nothing else and nothing less than the heart—than a true heart."[3] Friends, if we want to experience more of the kingdom, we must let God do heart surgery, no matter how daunting it may seem. But here is the good news: when our heavenly Father is the surgeon, there's no risk of human error or incompetence.

The surgery will be successful!

But it doesn't end there. This new heart is a container that God wants to fill. Let's look back at Ezekiel 36:26-27: "I will give you a new heart and put a new spirit in you; I will remove from you your heart of stone and give you a heart of flesh. And I will put my Spirit in you and move you to follow my decrees and be careful to keep my laws." When God gives you a new heart, he also gives you a new spirit. And it's not just any spirit. It's *his* Spirit. Stop and think about that for a moment. The Creator of the universe has put his Spirit within you! He is making you a holy vessel. He is giving you a purpose, and he wants you to be a carrier of his love.

Questions for Reflection

1. Is there something you feel that's missing from your spiritual life? Peace? Joy? Assurance? Purpose?

2. Can you describe a time you've experienced an emotional response (such as tears or laughter) to God's touch? (Please note that an emotional response isn't necessary in order to receive, but it can sometimes be a useful indicator.)

3. Reflect for a few moments on the word "abundance." What do you think God's abundance looks like in your life? Where would you like to see more of it?

Going Deeper

Ask your Father what gift he would like to give you today. He may give you a word or a picture. Meditate on the meaning of that gift in your life. **Describe how the gift makes you feel.**

I came that they may have life and have it abundantly.

— JOHN 10:10 *(ESV)*

CHAPTER 10

RECEIVING GOD'S LOVE

"God's love for us is everlasting. That means that God's love for us existed before we were born and will exist after we have died. It is an eternal love in which we are embraced."

— HENRI NOUWEN,
BREAD FOR THE JOURNEY

What does it really look like to live without fear?

I suppose very few of us ever see the completion of that kind of freedom this side of heaven. Of course, we can look to the giants in faith, who seemed to operate outside of fear, but sometimes it's hard to relate. John Wesley's story isn't yours, and neither is Heidi Baker's. But there is one common factor among those who find freedom from fear: an encounter with God's love.

The writings of Julian of Norwich have captivated me for years. A late fourteenth-century English mystic, Julian writes about her encounter with the love of God during a serious illness. I can remember how little I understood of this profound love the first time I picked up her book, *Revelations of Divine Love*. Looking back at my original notes, I spent most of my time marking areas I thought were theologically problematic. My heart was so closed I could only approach her writing with my head. But the head without connection to the heart is only capable of a black-and-white, right versus wrong analysis. My head was missing the bigger picture. I had not yet discovered the meaning of revelation, and I did not understand that Julian's writing contained something to be received.

And yet, while this all-encompassing love of which she spoke was nearly incomprehensible to me, I knew it was something I wanted to experience. The comfort Julian derives from her encounters, or "showings," revealed to me a lack of depth and intimacy in my relationship with God. The crux of the problem was my failure to understand God's love. My head could quote scripture as proof that God loved me, but my heart had yet to experience the reality of that love.

Julian writes, "Some of us believe that God is almighty, and can do everything; and that he is all wise, and may do everything; but that he is all love, and will do everything— there we draw back."[1] I knew I had drawn back and withheld my heart, but God honored my desire to go deeper and experience him more fully. Twenty years later, upon revisiting Julian's writing, I was struck by how much more I understood. Parts I previously dismissed as unfathomable took on new meaning as

I experienced greater depths of God's comfort and assurance.

The significance of the relationship between heart connection and true rest is something Julian understood because of her personal encounter. "I cannot tell the reality of Him who is my Maker, Lover and Keeper, for until I am united to Him in substance, I may never have complete rest or real bliss, that is, until I am so fastened to Him that there is absolutely no created thing between my God and me."[2] And so, this becomes our goal: to attach ourselves to God's very substance, which is the fullness of love, with no barrier between our heart and his.

Keep in mind everyone's journey is unique. Please don't waste time weighing your journey against someone else's. Judgment, even self-judgment, isn't your job. We all have our difficulties. We each have different areas of weakness. But God knows our fears and our weaknesses, and he is always willing to help us step into freedom.

We don't have to sort ourselves out first. If you wait until you've sorted out your issues before giving God access to your heart, you will miss out on what he has for you right now. Let's be honest, you can't really sort yourself out without him anyway, so surrender is the best path no matter where you find yourself. He meets us right where we are on the journey and can work with anything we lay at his feet. He wants to possess our hearts with his love, and he won't give up. As our trust grows, it becomes easier to lay more of our heart before him, allowing him to remove the things that stand between our heart and his. This is a lifelong process of infinite worth.

It is important to understand that none of this requires great intellectual fortitude or mental assent. You don't need to be C. S. Lewis or Dallas Willard, although we can all surely gain wisdom from such giants. God doesn't expect you to be an expert on Christian doctrine or have a thought life that never gets mired in the mundane. Rather, he simply desires to embrace you with his all-consuming love. In all things, his love is enough.

CఇS

Recently, I had a dream that I was in a place with a bubonic plague outbreak. (Remember the Black Death that swept across Europe in the Middle Ages? Yeah, *that* kind of plague.) In the dream, I was terrified of ants that were said to be spreading the plague. At one point, stranded on a grassy hill, separated from my family, I realized I needed to walk through the grass to where my husband was calling to me. Nothing about it looked dangerous, but I couldn't stop thinking about the grass—and the ants! Plague isn't actually spread by ants, but by rodents, fleas, and people, so I have no idea why ants were in my dream. Then I looked down and realized I was barefoot. Suddenly, what should have been an easy walk from one hilltop to another seemed utterly impossible.

For most people, bubonic plague is not something to worry about. You probably can't name a friend or family member who has had the plague. However, our family does mission in Madagascar, which is the only nation in the world that still has frequent outbreaks of the plague. When we prepared to book our flights for our most recent trip to Madagascar, there was a significant outbreak. I confess I felt a little uneasy with the ongoing quarantine situation in the area where we would be working. My husband had no qualms. He was ready to go ahead. But I wanted to see the next update from the World Health Organization before making a decision. In the end, our friends in Madagascar assured us the outbreak was waning, so we booked our trip.

What I believe God highlighted through the dream were areas of fear in my life I still needed his love to penetrate. I'm not beating myself up about this. I don't see myself as a failure because there are still lingering fears. This is just where I am on my journey, and that's okay. More recently, I've experienced moments of anxiety because of the global pandemic. Perhaps you can relate? I have many friends and family who have recovered from the virus, but it's still one of those *what-ifs* that I must regularly surrender to God.

One of the most fearless people I know is a missionary friend who worked in Madagascar. Her heart was so full of love for the children in her care that she actually stayed in the plague ward of the hospital overnight, sharing a bed with one of her beautiful girls who had contracted the plague. As I wrestled with whether to purchase plane tickets, she sent photos from the plague ward. Her love and courage left me in awe.

We may not all reach that level of fearlessness in our own journey, but we can take steps further into freedom. 1 John 4:18 reminds us that "the one who fears has not been made perfect in love." I know I've not yet been made perfect, but I also know I have a Father who gives lavishly (1 John 3:1). His love is infinite and always available. The more I let him touch my heart, the more love I receive. It's actually pretty simple, but it's easy to get caught up in our heads trying to force a change in ourselves.

I want to be completely clear, God's Word is powerful. It is truth. But berating yourself with the truth isn't the way to change your heart. As Dallas Willard so wisely said, "The will is transformed by experience, not information."[3] Heart transformation only happens through love. Once we have received his incredible love in our hearts, then we can understand what it means to have our minds renewed. For me, it was as if the power grid had suddenly switched on in my mind. I didn't just know certain scripture passages; I was truly understanding them.

Your Father wants to meet you right where you are on your journey. Remember how Thomas wasn't with the other disciples when Jesus first appeared to them after the resurrection? He hadn't seen Jesus with his own eyes, and he wasn't willing to believe. Yet, Jesus knew his struggle and met him in that place. He didn't heap condemnation on him. He simply met him in his place of doubt (John 20:24-29). And he wants to meet you in your place of doubt. He wants to shine his light in the darkness. He wants to show you that his perfect love really does cast out fear. So as you prepare to take the next steps on your journey into freedom, take to heart the words that Jesus spoke to his disciples: "Peace I leave with you; My peace I give to you. I do not give to you as the world gives. Do not let your hearts be troubled; do not be afraid" (John 14:27).

God is for you, not against you, on this journey. Your desire for freedom is absolutely his will. He wants you to be free to experience the abundant life that is available to you this side of heaven. A passage that illustrates this perfectly is Ephesians 1:17-19:

I keep asking that the God of our Lord Jesus Christ, the glorious Father, may give you the Spirit of wisdom and revelation, so that you may know him better. I pray that the eyes of your heart may be enlightened in order that you may know the hope to which he has called you, the riches of his glorious inheritance in his holy people, and his incomparably great power for us who believe.

This is my prayer for you: that you receive the heart revelation he has for you. This is not just a concept or hopeful conjecture, but an impartation of something real and substantial—something that will change you in ways you never imagined. It is, without a doubt, part of God's plan for you. When the eyes of your heart are enlightened, nothing looks the same anymore. From this new perspective, the impossible begins to look reasonable.

If you do nothing else after reading this book, seek this revelation. Your loving Father delights to give good gifts to those who ask (Matt 7:11). Give him access to your heart. He knows your needs better than you do. The fullness of this revelation will come in his timing. Resist the temptation to compare your journey to anyone else's. Your heart is your own, and so is your journey. You are unique and precious in God's eyes, and he will take you on the path he has chosen just for you.

As you continue to seek this revelation of God's love, be patient with yourself. Give yourself grace. You will not figure it all out at once, and you don't have to. It's much easier to accept that you are like a little kid who is still learning. You will make mistakes. Even as you gain freedom, there will be times when you'll slip into your old mode of fearful reactions. It's okay. You have a Father who doesn't condemn you. He will pick you up when you fall and remind you of his love for you. That's who he is. Be gentle with yourself and let him lead you. His path is so much better.

If you long to receive more of God's love, he will not leave you disappointed. As I look back now, I see that from the moment I prayed for more, he answered that prayer. I didn't see it as first, but he was gradually softening the soil of my heart. My hardened heart couldn't handle a flood, so the process looked more like a slow drip. God knew what was best. Once my heart was suitably prepared, he released as much of the flood as I could handle. But there is always more. His love is a reservoir that has no bottom. We can always go deeper.

I love this prayer that Andrew Murray includes in his book
With Christ in the School of Prayer. If you feel stuck or unsure
how to move forward, this is a great place to start:

> *Blessed Father! You are love, and only he who*
> *dwells in love can come into fellowship with You.*
> *Your blessed Son has taught me again how deeply*
> *true this is. O my God! Let the Holy Spirit flood*
> *my heart with your love. Be a fountain of love*
> *inside me that flows out to everyone around me.*
> *Let the power of believing prayer spring out of this*
> *life of love. O my Father! Grant by the Holy Spirit*
> *that this love may be the gate through which I find*
> *life in Your love. Let the joy with which I daily*
> *forgive whomever might offend me be the proof*
> *that Your forgiveness is my power and life.*
>
> *Lord Jesus! Blessed Teacher! Teach me how to*
> *forgive and to love. Let the power of your blood*
> *make the pardon of my sins a reality, so that your*
> *forgiveness of me and my forgiveness of others may*
> *be the very joy of heaven. Point out the weak-*
> *nesses in my relationships with others that might*
> *hinder my fellowship with God. May my daily*
> *life at home and in society be the school in which*
> *strength and confidence are gathered for the prayer*
> *of faith. Amen.*[4]

What a beautifully humble prayer. When we ask our heavenly Father for more of his love, he gives willingly. You don't have to wrench God's love out of his hands. It's yours for the taking. But if you have trouble believing that God would do this for you, let me add my faith to yours. I've been there—needing someone to come alongside me, to be like the friends in Luke 5 who lowered the paralytic man through the roof so he could be healed. If you are reading this, I'm believing for you. I know in my heart it is God's will for you to receive the impartation of his love.

But this is not a revelation you receive through striving. This journey is not about *doing*. It is about *being*. Revelation comes through surrender. Henri Nouwen recounts his journey into the Father's heart this way:

> *I cannot make myself feel loved... I cannot bring myself home nor can I create communion on my own. I can desire it, hope for it, wait for it, yes, pray for it. But my true freedom I cannot fabricate for myself. That must be given to me.*[5]

For me, this process has felt like receiving a new foundation. If you are like me, you recognize life has made some serious cracks and blown a few sizable holes in the foundation of your heart. There's rubble and deep fissures that hinder your attempts at stability and growth. But God wants to take that rubble and repurpose it. He wants to fill the cracks and chasms with his love. It's his work, not ours, but we have to allow him into the deepest places in our heart. He needs full access, and the excavation process can be uncomfortable. As Watchman Nee observed, "The Spirit is both a builder and a dweller. He cannot dwell where he has not built; He builds to dwell and dwells in only what he has built."[6]

This process of reconstruction requires us to take a hard look at pains we've hidden deeply or chosen to ignore. It may prompt us to ask questions about emotions that rise to the surface. *Where did that come from? Why am I feeling this way?* It even makes us wonder if the process is worth it. But whatever emotions are stirred up by the healing process—anger, fear, sorrow, shame—resist the temptation to condemn yourself for experiencing them or to shove them back down. C. S. Lewis wrote, "No natural feelings are high or low, holy or unholy, in themselves. They are all holy when God's hand is on the rein. They all go bad when they set up on their own and make themselves into false gods."[7] Simply name the emotions that arise and put them in safe hands. It is important to remember the One who loves you most is with you in the process.

Jesus is rooting for your breakthrough. He's actively sorting through the rubble and making something new while he fills the holes that let love leak out. And when you discover God's love has filled in all those cracks, you will experience his love in a new way. Without the leaky places, God's love rises within you. It overflows in such a way that it affects those around you. You become more like the one who is healing your heart because he is remaking you in his image.

og

A few years ago, my husband and I had the opportunity to pray for a young girl in Africa. Grace lived in a children's home and had a history of sexual abuse. She was acting out toward the other children in her home, so her caregivers asked if we would pray for her. Having recently experienced an increased flow of God's love, we approached this time of prayer with Grace as an opportunity to step out of the way and let our Father's love bring transformation.

We sat with Grace in the small bedroom of a local missionary's home and began to pray. We felt strongly we should not have our prayers translated, so we asked the translator to leave. For the next hour and a half, we simply prayed love over Grace. She had no idea what we were saying, but love is a language of its own. As I held her on my lap, the prayers took hold, and I could feel her small body relaxing. She softened against me, and I noticed tears welling up in her eyes. I had the sense that she needed a father's embrace, so I placed her in my husband's arms and we continued to pray. Almost immediately, she turned her face into his chest and sobbed. We held her for some time, unable to restrain our own tears.

As the sun began to set, her caregivers returned to take her home for dinner. But Grace wasn't the least bit interested in dinner, or popcorn, or the Disney movies her caregivers offered. She clung to my husband's leg with all the strength her tiny arms could muster. While my husband and I were only vessels,

Grace had experienced the overflow of God's love, and she had no desire to leave. Who could blame her? Our time with Grace was a precious moment in which we experienced the intensity of our Father's love for one little girl. I wouldn't trade those ninety minutes for anything. But perhaps the most amazing part of the story is the transformation that occurred in Grace.

We've been back to visit a few times over the last three years. Each time Grace has welcomed us with hugs. She's held our hands and danced with us during church services, seeming happy and well-adjusted. She's not clingy, but confident. Her caregivers report that the specific behavior problem for which they initially brought her to us is no longer an issue. Grace is a perfect example of how we can be changed by an encounter with love.

The time with Grace deepened my conviction that God's love can move mountains. When I pray for others, I need only get out of the way, and allow his love to flow. I don't want to minister from any other place than standing firmly in the center of God's love. And what a privilege to be a vessel for the very substance of God.

Questions for Reflection

1. What scripture passages do you *know* with your head that you would like to *understand* with your heart?

2. Describe a time in your life when you have experienced God's peace? What led to that experience? (Was it prayer, scripture, God's creation, an encouraging word, an embrace from a friend, or something else?)

3. What are some ways you enjoy spending time with God? What makes those times special?

Going Deeper

Ask God to direct you to a passage of scripture he would like to reveal to you in a new way. Ask him to speak to your heart. **Read the passage and wait for his revelation.**

May the Lord direct your hearts to the love of God and to the steadfastness of Christ.

— 2 Thessalonians 3:5 *(ESV)*

CHAPTER 11

GETTING PRACTICAL

*"Suppose our failures occur, not in spite of what we
are doing, but precisely because of it."*

— DALLAS WILLARD,
THE DIVINE CONSPIRACY

Beloved, there is nothing you can do to make God love you
more. And there is nothing you can do to make him love you
less. These are essential truths that have proven difficult for
many Christians (myself included) to believe. Can God really
love us that much? That sounds too good to be true. So we
spend our lives trying to earn God's love or prevent him from
not loving us. Praying, reading scripture, serving in church
or the community—these are great, but they won't make our
heavenly Father love us more than he already does. He wants
to pour his love into our hearts, but there are many things we
do that can actually prevent it from happening. Being busy for
God may be a way to convince ourselves we've got it right, but
God doesn't want our busyness. He wants our hearts.

The more I stay present in the moment, the more I see what God is doing. If I distract myself with a thousand "worthy" tasks, I miss out on what he has chosen for me. If I am constantly replaying moments from my past that I regret, I can't see where he is working in my life today. If I spend my time planning and strategizing for the future, I don't hear what he is saying now. That doesn't mean there isn't a time for planning. And of course, there are tasks that need to be done. But we need to leave room for relationship and space for encounter.

So how can we create that space? Slowing down is a great place to start, and that will probably require you to let some things fall through the cracks. I know this can be hard to swallow, but perfectionism is not your friend. You cannot be all things to all people, and God doesn't expect you to be. Letting go of things that keep you trapped in busyness is essential to creating space for divine encounter.

Even some of our spiritual practices can amount to busyness when our heart is not yielded. Deep personal reflection is valuable, but it means more than just reading your Bible. It is possible to read God's Word day after day and never experience heart change. That was my experience for many years, and I didn't understand why. I learned about God as I read (and that is not without value), but my heart was not positioned to receive. I was stuck in a *doing* mindset, which told me I was responsible for creating heart change.

Ultimately, I had to stop adopting everyone's spiritual quick fixes. All the Christian self-help books and Bible reading plans in the world would never achieve heart healing for me if I never let my Father get close to my heart. I needed to recognize the way he speaks to me and allow a genuine relationship to grow. I needed to experience his love, not just read about it. Only God knew the unique way to touch my heart, and that process took time. As Dallas Willard has said, "Recognizing God's voice is something [we] must learn to do through [our] own personal experience and experimentation."[1]

You may want to ask yourself a few questions. What activities bring you joy? What do you truly love to do that doesn't come from a place of striving? What makes you feel like a kid again? Or what is something you've always wanted to try but have never had the confidence to take the first step toward doing? The answers to these questions may give you some ideas about fresh ways you can encounter God's love. When we step out of our comfort zone and trust God to guide us in a new endeavor or join us in a long forgotten passion, we experience him in surprising ways. We may even experience him rekindling our sense of childlike wonder.

Before I offer some practical ideas, I want to reiterate that there is no magic formula, no list of rules you must follow. God is only seeking an open heart. How you are best able to create space and open your heart is entirely unique to you. God will not withhold himself from you if you don't adhere to a particular contemplative practice. I tried for many years to be one of those people who love their early morning quiet time. The problem was I didn't love it, and I felt guilty about not loving it. Once I realized I could experience precious time with God any time of the day, I felt a new freedom. It's not as though sitting in my window seat with my Bible, journal, and a cup of tea at 3:00 p.m. was any less worthy than it would be at 6:00 a.m. Morning isn't somehow more holy than afternoon. God made all the hours of the day. What matters is identifying your own unique way of aligning your heart with God's so that you can be filled.

CB

Throughout much of my life, music has been my primary form of artistic expression. Strangely, when worship groups were being formed among our fellow students during our three months in New Zealand, I felt no inclination to join. Normally, that would be my thing. But I had the sense that if I took a role in leading worship, I'd set myself up for an unhealthy battle with striving and performance, which were the last things I needed to deal with at that time.

Having performed for much of my childhood in a professional children's chorus, and having studied vocal music in college, it is difficult for me to separate music from performance. I have struggled to detach myself from the striving and perfectionism that was such a part of my younger self. For this reason, other than occasionally writing music or dabbling at the piano, I will usually draw or dance when I want to express what God has put on my heart. These are two areas of creativity in which I have more ability to just flow, without placing expectations on myself. I have more freedom to simply *be* when I am dancing or drawing with God, and it brings me joy. Perhaps you find this freedom in other activities like cooking, gardening, or writing. What calms your spirit and brings you joy?

Another way I can easily enter into a receiving posture is by encountering God in creation. This is just the way I am wired. My happiest memories from childhood involve walks in the woods, climbing trees, and picking spring flowers around our farm. When I think of those things, peace comes upon me. I can still remember being overcome with the majesty of the Cascade Mountains on my first trip to the Pacific Northwest when I was thirteen. I had a cheap camera that couldn't do justice to the scenery, but I used all my film trying to capture a sense of what I perceived in my spirit. I wanted to preserve that sense of wonder.

Even before I was a Christian, it was nature that convinced me of God's existence. Now, when I need reminders of his greatness, I seek out his creation and meet with him there. Perhaps you have a special place where you like to meet with God. If you don't, ask him to show you one. I have a few special places, some I can easily get to and others, like a waterfall in New Zealand, that I can't. But the places we can't physically get to can still be places where we meet with Jesus. Close your eyes and envision that place. Now ask Jesus to join you there. Ask him what he would like to show you or say to you. Just enjoy his presence. No expectations. No demands. There's no right or wrong way to do it.

I know many people who connect with God while running or biking or enjoying some other endurance exercise. The rhythm of the physical activity clears the mind and creates space to hear from God. I'm not much of an athlete, so I can't say I have experience with that. Usually, when I'm running, my thoughts are consumed with how I'm going to finish without collapsing. However, if you are more athletically inclined, I encourage you to see how this works for you.

I've also found that taking time to reflect upon God's promises, while giving thanks for the ways I've seen him move in my life, helps me align my heart to his. This bolsters my faith, especially when circumstances are difficult. But this doesn't mean we pretend everything is rosy. We can be vulnerable with God, and it's okay to ask hard questions amid trials. *Where are you, Lord? Do you even hear me? Why don't you answer?* God doesn't get angry when we honestly bare our hearts to him. Even the most faith-filled Christians have these moments. We're human, and God loves us even in our human weakness. Throughout the Psalms, we see this honest outpouring of the heart coupled with recognition of God's faithfulness. Psalm 77:1-12 provides a wonderful example:

> *"I cried out to God for help;*
> *I cried out to God to hear me.*

When I was in distress, I sought the Lord;
at night I stretched out untiring hands,
and I would not be comforted.

I remembered you, God, and I groaned;
I meditated, and my spirit grew faint.

You kept my eyes from closing;
I was too troubled to speak.
I thought about the former days,
the years of long ago;
I remembered my songs in the night.
My heart meditated and my spirit asked:

"Will the Lord reject forever?
Will he never show his favor again?
Has his unfailing love vanished forever?
Has his promise failed for all time?
Has God forgotten to be merciful?
Has he in anger withheld his compassion?"

Then I thought, "To this I will appeal:
the years when the Most High stretched out his
right hand.
I will remember the deeds of the Lord;
yes, I will remember your miracles of long ago.
I will consider all your works
and meditate on all your mighty deeds."

When we despair that God is absent, it is helpful to recount his goodness and remember what he has *already* done for us. Hope springs from trusting in God's character, even when our circumstances appear hopeless. It is harder to doubt when we acknowledge how he has been faithful.

Psalm 44 is a communal lament in which the Psalmist recalls Israel's many victories wrought by the Lord.

> *It was not by their sword that they won the land,*
> *nor did their arm bring them victory;*
> *it was your right hand, your arm*
> *and the light of your face, for you loved them.*

> —PSALM 44:3

I love the way this verse acknowledges we are not the ones who bring about victory. We are not the ones fighting the battle. The Psalmist's perspective is a reminder we can trust in God's love when we are struggling. And yet, the psalm turns darker in verse 9: "But now you have rejected and humbled us; you no longer go out with our armies."

Wait. What? Wasn't the Psalmist just praising God for his faithfulness? This change in tone feels so human. Have you been in that place? Everything is going along just fine. Life is great and God is in your corner. Then suddenly you're knocked down by disappointment or despair. It feels like you've been punched in the gut. *Where are you, God? I thought you were fighting for me.*

Again, there's nothing wrong with laying our sorrow and disappointment before God. Psalm 44 ends in lament, but we know this isn't the end of the story. Did God stop fighting for Israel once Psalm 44 was penned? Of course not. Like the Israelites, we can feel that God has turned his back on us, but that's never the truth. He doesn't leave us (Joshua 1:5), and he won't hide his face from us. "I will no longer hide my face from them, for I will pour out my Spirit on the house of Israel" (Ezekiel 39:29). We who follow Jesus have been filled with his Spirit. This is something the ancient Israelites did not experience. For those who are in Christ, there is truly no way to flee from his presence. He is both *with* and *in* us. But like the Israelites, sometimes we need to remind our fearful selves that he is there—that he fights for us, and his love indwells us.

Years ago, as I waited for God to deliver me from physical pain and the accompanying fog of fear, I felt the Lord gently tell me I should have something tangible as a reminder of the ways he answered my prayers. As I considered some sort of physical item to help me focus on God's goodness and faithfulness, I was led to Joshua 4. Here I found the story of the Israelites at long last crossing into the promised land as God stopped the flood waters of the Jordan to allow his people safe passage. This was no average day. God had done a great miracle, and his people were finally home. But what jumped off the page was the Lord's command to Joshua, which is carried out by twelve of his men. Joshua tells them:

Go over before the ark of the LORD your God

into the middle of the Jordan. Each of you is to
take up a stone on his shoulder, according to the
number of the tribes of the Israelites, to serve as a
sign among you. In the future, when your children
ask you, 'What do these stones mean?' tell them
that the flow of the Jordan was cut off before the
ark of the covenant of the LORD. When it crossed
the Jordan, the waters of the Jordan were cut off.
These stones are to be a memorial to the people of
Israel forever.

— JOSHUA 4:5-7

Why does the Lord tell the Israelites to do this? Because they are human and forgetful, just like us. During trials, it is easy to forget the ways God has come through for us in the past. When fear grips us, we wonder if he hears our cries. How could I forget he had healed my husband of life-threatening allergies? How could I forget he gave me two beautiful children? Yet it can be so easy to forget what God has done for us. When we wander away from our true home and into fear, we need to be found by the One who is love. Henri Nouwen suggests, "We can allow ourselves to be found by God and healed by his love through the concrete and daily practice of trust and gratitude."² When we remember what he has done, life-giving faith rises within our spirit.

I took the passage in Joshua 4 to heart and decided I wanted to have a pendant with twelve stones I could wear every day as a sign of God's faithfulness. This was the early 2000s, before online shopping was as easy as it is today, so I went on quite a search. Eventually, I found a beautiful rectangular silver pendant inlaid with twelve semiprecious stones. I didn't realize it at the time, but it is a representation of Aaron's breastplate.

The store was in Jerusalem, and they weren't able to accept online payment. I was determined to purchase the pendant, so I called the jeweler directly. Her English was a little better than my Hebrew, but we somehow figured it out. A couple weeks later, I placed the silver chain and pendant around my neck as a constant reminder of God's love for his people, which included me. When doubt or fear rose to the surface, I would simply touch my necklace as a reminder that I have a heavenly Father who keeps his promises.

I'm not saying you need to buy a piece of jewelry, but something you can touch during times of fear or doubt can be useful. Maybe a heart-shaped stone or a small wooden cross. Just ask God to highlight something that would be meaningful to you.

03

Journaling is another great way to reflect on God's faithfulness. I'll confess to being a sporadic journaler, but I find it a life-giving practice. I love to write questions I have for God and wait in stillness for him to speak to my heart. Then I write what I believe he is saying. This often involves a scripture passage, but not always. Sometimes it's just a phrase or a profound sense of peace. Once, in response to a question about a chaotic situation, I simply heard, *Look for the light.* I took time to reflect on those words and let God reveal a deeper meaning. Months later I was amazed to go back to that entry and see how God continued to work in the situation.

My husband is more consistent with journaling than I am. It has become his primary way of hearing from God. Over the years, his journals have become remarkable conversations that convey vast amounts of wisdom and love. His intimacy with God has increased exponentially through their beautiful exchange, and he is blessed to have a record of this relationship.

If you are new to journaling, take some time to explore the different journals available. I enjoy a beautiful hardback with space to write and draw. I've even purchased solid-colored journals and decorated the cover with paint pens. I like to feel the journal is a unique expression of my heart. If you're not sure how to start, you could explore guided journals that provide prompts or exercises to help you listen and receive. You may be amazed at how this simple act creates an opening for God to move in your heart.

Another wonderful tool for receiving is soaking prayer. If you are not familiar with this, think of it as a time of meditation in which you simply rest in God's presence and soak in his love. Honestly, this is one of my favorite ways to pray. At my lowest point in the struggle with autoimmune disease, this was the only way I could find peace. It required absolutely nothing from me at a time when I had nothing to give. All I needed was a comfortable place to lie down, maybe a pillow and blanket, and some soothing music. I would often allow myself to drift into sleep, trusting that my active participation was unnecessary for God to work. If he wanted to get my attention, he could certainly do so through dreams—and sometimes he did.

I went to soaking prayer sessions offered by various ministries, but I would also lie down at home while playing music specifically written for soaking. I had one recording of someone reading all the passages in scripture about love. I found that to be a powerful way to increase my awareness of God's presence and position myself to receive. There are many good resources available for soaking, and I have built an extensive playlist over the years. The key is to find something that brings you peace. Look around on the internet, and you'll find something that works for you.

It's worth mentioning that there are many useful and praiseworthy materials found on the internet, but we must exercise discernment in this area. Much of what exists on the web can be toxic. As you look for helpful spiritual practices, don't veer off into the weeds. As someone who has struggled with fear, I've learned that endless web searches for answers rarely helped. God is my healer, not Google.

Recently, I was praying with a good friend who has dealt

with chronic illness for several years. God has given her an incredible revelation of his love. She has experienced a significant amount of healing, but she's holding on to a promise of greater breakthrough. We discussed the difficulty of keeping your eyes fixed on Jesus during trials. I shared with her how easily I stepped out of love and into fear whenever I searched for solutions on the internet.

As we prayed, I saw the image of a spider web. As an insect flies into the web, tiny strands stick to it. It doesn't seem like a big deal, but the more the insect moves, the more it gets entangled. The insect is bound and becomes prey. Isn't that an interesting image of how we, often unintentionally, open ourselves up to the enemy? A simple Google search about a troubling symptom prompts us to click on one link, then another. It doesn't seem like much, but suddenly fear pounces.

It is important to remember that while we are not the ones who defeat fear, we have daily choices about where to fix our eyes. God fights for us, but our position matters. With the wisdom of the Holy Spirit, we can discern what is helpful as we step out from fear's grip and into abiding love. By God's grace, we can receive all we need to withstand the storms that come our way.

I don't want you to be confused about what I'm saying here. It's so easy for those of us who struggle with fear to become enslaved by a judgment mindset, constantly worrying about making the "right" decisions and avoiding the "wrong" ones.

Instead, step back and ask the Father for more of his love each day. Ask the Holy Spirit to impart wisdom. Ask Jesus to protect you by his blood. These things are always in his will and available to his children. By asking these things, we are entrusting our decisions to the unfailing power of the Trinity. And even when we fail, there is grace.

Lastly, before turning to what living in God's spacious love looks like, I want to address another matter which has been a source of confusion for many Christians. I suspect some who read this book have sought counseling or therapy to help with the struggle against fear and anxiety. Perhaps you are currently seeing a counselor or therapist. Let me be very clear that I am not trying to give the impression that psychological counseling is unhelpful, or that there aren't times when antidepressant or antianxiety medications are necessary and helpful. Both avenues have been helpful to me.

If you take prescription medication to help with depression or anxiety, *do not let that be a source of shame in your life.* I've known far too many Christians who believe that "giving in" and taking medication means they have failed. This is a lie that the enemy loves to exploit. Can God heal someone to such an extent they can leave medication behind? Absolutely, but that may not be the case for everyone. We are all different and on our own journey. Some of us have very real biochemical issues that medication can help us overcome. Sometimes prescription drugs are helpful in getting us to a place where we can quiet our thoughts enough to receive the healing God has for us.

There is no shame in that. Regardless of whether you need medication, God is still the healer. Give yourself grace and always seek God's guidance. He wants the best for you.

Questions for Reflection

1. How does God speak to you? Do you hear a voice, experience a sudden thought or emotion, or perhaps notice his hand in something?

2. When do you feel closest to God? How do you know he is with you?

3. What practices or hobbies quiet your heart and allow you to receive? How often do you make time for these things?

Going Deeper

Make time today to be with God, whether walking outdoors, painting, or sitting quietly with him—anything that creates heart space. **Journal what he reveals to you in his presence.**

Finally, brothers and sisters, whatever is true, whatever is noble, whatever is right, whatever is pure, whatever is lovely, whatever is admirable—if anything is excellent or praiseworthy—think about such things. Whatever you have learned or received or heard from me, or seen in me—put it into practice. And the God of peace will be with you.

— Philippians 4:8-9

CHAPTER 12

LIVING IN THE SPACIOUS PLACE

*"Beloved, I say, let your fears go, lest they make you
fainthearted. Stop inspiring fear in those around you
and now take your stand in faith. God has been good
and He will continue to manifest His goodness. Let
us approach these days expecting to see the goodness
of the Lord manifest. Let us be strong and of good
courage, for the Lord will fight for us if we stand
in faith."*

— FRANCIS FRANGIPANE

Throughout my journey there was a word I repeatedly heard
from the Lord, and it comes from David's Song of Praise: "He
brought me out into a spacious pace; he rescued me because
he delighted in me" (2 Sam 22:20; Psalm 18:19 NIV). As I
looked into the text, I was led back to Exodus (and if you need
encouragement about God being able to lead you to freedom,
this is a great place to start). In Exodus 3:8, we read, "So I have

come down to rescue them from the hand of the Egyptians and to bring them up out of that land into a good and spacious land, a land flowing with milk and honey." I knew I needed deliverance from the land I was living in, so to speak. In my heart, I meditated on the meaning of these words. I accepted them as a promise that God would bring me out into a good and spacious land. That sure sounded appealing as there was nothing spacious about the box I felt trapped in.

One day, as I focused on God's promise to me, I saw myself in a tiny, dark place. It was that old familiar box. I cried out to God, asking him how I could get out. He told me to bend down and pick up what was on the floor. I couldn't see what was below me because the space was pitch black, but I bent down and felt a smooth ball. It was heavy, about the size of a bowling ball. I picked it up and asked God what I was supposed to do with it. I sensed he was telling me to throw it. Given the weight of the ball, I questioned this. I didn't think I could throw it far, and I didn't see what throwing it could accomplish. But I obeyed and threw the ball into the darkness.

The ball did not go very far, but it went far enough. Mere inches from my face, it tore through the wall of the box, which turned out to be only paper. The tear exposed a green meadow, blue skies, and bright sunlight. As the paper box crumpled to the ground, I realized I was standing in a spacious place that was warm and welcoming. I had actually been standing there all along. I just didn't know it. The darkness was only paper thin, but it had blinded me to the reality of God's love.

This image was significant for me. It illustrated the truth of God's promise to deliver me from fear, and it gave me something to envision on my journey. Freedom didn't come immediately, but I was in a better place to step out in faith, trusting God as my deliverer. When our view is not aligned with how God sees us, our world gets smaller and more limited. But God had shown me he was working on my heart and would bring me out into the light. He knew how to tear down the walls that surrounded me.

Following this encounter, when challenges arose and fear tried to overtake me, I would employ different methods of staying focused on the destination God had revealed. At times I felt led to do what I call a "symbolic fast." I ate and drank only things that symbolized God's promise. This included pita and grape juice representing the salvation I had received in Christ, and plain yogurt and honey representing the spacious land in Exodus 3:8. Other times, I would make artistic representations of God's promise to me. For instance, while my kids were at school, I would sit at the kitchen table and write words in calligraphy that kept me focused on reaching God's destination. One word I chose was the Hebrew word *shalem,* meaning "complete, safe, peaceful, perfect, whole." I would write the word and then draw colorful designs around it as I focused on the meaning. When I finished a drawing, I would tape it to our kitchen window as a present reminder that God was leading me out of the darkness.

These meditations and activities were helpful, and I believe

God used them to prepare my heart for the bigger work he wanted to do. I would love to say that after a year of symbolic fasting and drawing my heart out, I suddenly stepped into freedom, but it simply isn't true. God was softening the soil of my heart and clearing away weeds so, in his timing, I could receive a greater impartation of his love. I cannot emphasize enough that stepping into freedom is a process. In our culture of instant gratification, we're all looking for a quick fix. We want the answers now, and patience can be a real challenge, but it is essential to understand our journey from the eternal perspective.

As Christians, we have already entered into the eternal, even though we must still live our present lives within temporal constraints. What feels like a long time to us is but a moment to God. Our omniscient God sees our struggles and suffering, and he doesn't minimize our experience. In his flesh, Jesus experienced the same suffering and temporal struggles that we face. His compassion is limitless. He isn't just *with* us as we journey through the dark places; he is *in* us and never stops loving us. Hebrews 4 reminds us that, like the ancient Israelites, we are to observe a sabbath rest. But because we are in Christ, rest is not simply a day to cease from work, it is an eternal condition. When the One who is rest dwells within us, and we in him, our striving ends. Sabbath isn't just a day, but a way of life—kingdom life.

We can look to the life of a seventeenth-century French monk as an excellent illustration. Brother Lawrence's profound reflections in *The Practice of the Presence of God* offer a window into the heart of someone who discovered that true union with Christ brings rest and peace at all times. He recounts how he could experience God's love at work in the monastery kitchen, just as he could during intentional times of prayer. In one letter he recounts, "For my part I keep myself retired with Him in the depth or center of my soul as much as I can; and while I am so with Him I fear nothing, but the least turning from Him is insupportable."[1] Keeping our focus trained on God is important, but even this is accomplished with his help and through his love.

It's easy to forget that we are placed within the One who is rest. Life gets busy and stressful, but even in the work we must do, it is possible for our spirit to remain at rest. I know this may seem absurd when your inbox is exploding with urgent messages, or you're trying to cook dinner and the kids are trying to kill each other, but God is nearer than you think. This is really my heart for you: that you will discover God's rest in the spacious place he has prepared for you. A couple years ago, I started a blog called *The Spacious Place,* and I still don't know any better description of what I have discovered the further I've stepped into God's love.

CB

We already know we can't manufacture patience. Patience flows from God's love. When filled with his love, it is much easier to trust his timeline. We begin to see things from his eternal perspective. Little fears that goad us from day-to-day disappear. Bigger fears wither and lose their power as our lives take on a different rhythm.

Living in the spacious place also means giving ourselves grace by stepping out of self-judgment and condemnation. Your heavenly Father isn't staring down at you from his throne, waiting for you to slip up. Hebrews 4:16 tells us we can "approach God's throne of grace with confidence, so that we may receive mercy and find grace to help us in our time of need." Similarly, Ephesians 3:12 says, "In him and through faith in him we may approach God with freedom and confidence." From this place, we think about God differently. Our faith increases because we trust in his goodness. Peace and joy become more than fleeting moments that only bubble up from time to time. They become foundational, constant. Extending grace to others feels more natural as it becomes harder to take offense. Forgiveness becomes easier, more like a reflex. In short, we understand that what we carry is infinitely greater than anything coming against us. This is the beginning of freedom.

Have you ever wished you could pursue a dream without worrying what others would say? Have you longed to take a risk without fear of failure? Love gives us the freedom to be fully who we were created to be. We don't need someone else's validation for our creativity or adventure. As we partner with love, we are enabled to take risks and make discoveries. We also become catalysts for transformation in others. It's a radically different way to live.

Does living in the spacious place mean our lives are suddenly perfect? Of course not. We still live in a broken world, and there is an undeniable tension in that. There are moments when I feel darkness closing in around me, especially when I sense a general atmosphere of fear. Perhaps you've also noticed this during the global pandemic. It is easy to pick up fear and step into darkness when people around you dwell there. But now I know that darkness is not my reality. I have a different perspective. My feet have found a better foundation, which makes it easier to stand firm and tell the darkness to back off. Before receiving a heart revelation of God's love, the darkness felt like my home. As much as I didn't want to live there, I wasn't aware that there was another option—an infinitely better option. But God, through his love and mercy, showed me my true home.

From my first glimpse of the spacious place to the moment I stepped into greater freedom, God was constantly working. He knew the order in which my healing needed to proceed. When he showed me my destination, it gave me hope. Although it took several years for me to realize the freedom I experience today, he showed me the small, dark box was a lie, a tool of the enemy to keep me trapped in fear. But now I know where I belong. Even when I feel myself slipping into fear, I know I have an anchor. He will not let me go. He continues to fight for me. The rest he offers in his heart is my true home.

Recently, I struggled with some negative comments I received about one of my blog posts. The comments came from someone I knew. She took offense at what I had written, and I didn't know why. That old familiar fear of rejection raised its ugly head, but I handled it differently than I once would have. Instead of wallowing in it, as I was prone to do, I asked God why her comments stung so much, why they felt like a personal rejection. He reminded me that the person who made the comments was dealing with her own fears and disappointments. With that understanding, I prayed for her. That simple decision changed my perspective. Instead of focusing on my hurt, I acted in love toward the one who hurt me.

Self-condemnation also threatened to grab hold of me as I pondered what I had written. When I write, my intent is to bring healing, so the idea I'd hurt someone didn't sit well with me. If I'm not careful, it can be an open door to the small, dark box. I asked God about what I had written. Had I been insensitive? I knew my question was coming from a place of insecurity, and God knew this too. He reminded me I had prayed before I posted my blog and that my intent was for good. He didn't condemn me, and I didn't need to condemn myself. I had not stepped out of his love. He had not rejected me. In that moment, he led me to Psalm 37:3-7:

> *Trust in the Lord and do good;*
> *dwell in the land and enjoy safe pasture.*
> *Delight yourself in the Lord*
> *and he will give you the desires of your heart.*
>
> *Commit your way to the Lord;*

trust in him and he will do this:
He will make your righteousness
shine like the dawn, the justice of your cause
like the noonday sun.

Be still before the Lord and wait
patiently for him...

As I continued to read, I noticed a theme of inheritance. Verse 9 states, "But those who hope in the Lord will inherit the land." I saw it again in verses 22, 29, and 34. This is truly God's heart for us. He has good and eternal things for his beloved. Land that is spacious and fruitful. Streams that flow through arid land. Light that penetrates darkness. Love that dispels fear.

He has truly brought me to a place where I *can* trust him, with both my healing process and the outcome. I am free from having to figure it out myself. My part was simply to be open to the process, to surrender to the One who is love. I'm grateful to have entered a place where I am able to experience my inheritance, not just imagine what it might look like. We can enjoy the gifts he gives and the fruit he produces right now in this life. As Psalm 27:13 promises, "I will see the goodness of the Lord in the land of the living." For years, I didn't think that was possible. Perhaps you can relate? But consider this for a moment. I didn't enter by fighting my way through the door. I entered by surrendering and letting my Shepherd carry me. I discovered his rest, and this is my hope for you as well.

If God has begun this process in you, you may feel unsteady. It's challenging to adjust to a heart change, even when we know the change is good. I remember feeling a little like a puzzle box that someone had shaken up. The pieces were all in there, but they weren't yet in their proper place. Feeling confused and unsure is normal, but let me assure you that God won't leave you that way. Philippians 1:6 reminds us that "he who began a good work in you will carry it on to completion until the day of Christ Jesus." God finishes what he starts, and that's good news.

Beloved, "taste and see that the Lord is good. Blessed is the one who takes refuge in him" (Psalm 34:8). May he lead you to safe pasture—to the place where you can dwell without fear. May you discover the place where you are free to be who he created you to be, without fear of condemnation or rejection by man or God. As you continue to pursue him, may your righteousness shine like the dawn and be a beacon for others who struggle with fear. "Wait for the Lord; be strong and take heart and wait for the Lord" (Psalm 27:14).

What is the longing of your heart? This is an important question to ask yourself and answer honestly. When we are honest with ourselves and honest with God, he is more than willing to meet us where we are. It's why Jesus asked the man at the pool of Bethesda, "Do you want to get well?" It's a profound spiritual question, and our response matters to Jesus. Are we willing to enter into a new reality—a kingdom reality? Will we let him search our hearts? Do we want to let him tear down walls so we can step out into a spacious place? If this is the desire of your heart, you can trust Jesus, your heavenly Father, and the Holy Spirit to lead you there. All God requires is an open heart.

You are God's creation, his child. He made you to be a light in the darkness. He made you to be a vessel for his love. This is his purpose for you, and his plans will not be thwarted. As Freda Hanbury wrote in her poem, *Wait Thou Only Upon God*: "Stand still and see the victories thy God will gain for thee."

Questions for Reflection

1. Describe a time when you have felt trapped, enclosed, or smothered by fear? How did you step out of that place?

2. Reflect upon the feeling of being trapped by fear. How would the experience of living in freedom be different?

3. What has God shown you about the meaning and value of rest? What might true rest look like in your life?

Going Deeper

What does a spacious place look like to you? Describe it in words or draw a picture. **Dwell there for as long as you like while asking God to show you how he is loving you right now.**

A Final Suggestion...

Write a personal letter to your heavenly Father. Tell him your dreams and desires. Share your fears and anxieties with him. Thank him for loving you. Ask him to highlight areas of your heart that he wants to heal. Allow this letter to be the beginning of an intimate dialogue.

> *Come, all you who are thirsty, come to the waters; and you who have no money, come, buy and eat! Come, buy wine and milk without money and without cost. Why spend money on what is not bread, and your labor on what does not satisfy? Listen, listen to me, and eat what is good, and you will delight in the richest of fare. Give ear and come to me; listen, that you may live.*
>
> *— Isaiah 55:1-3*

EPILOGUE

Even as I complete the final edits for this book, I am given the opportunity to put these lessons into practice. My husband and I were exposed to Covid-19 this week. As we quarantine and wait, it would be easy to fall into fear. Last night, I felt it rising up. I knew I needed to position my heart to receive assurance from my heavenly Father. The fear tried to block my attempts at first, but as I continued to share my struggle with God, comfort came and the fear lifted. I will forever be grateful to have encountered this love that is like no other —a love that truly does cast out fear. I pray that you will also encounter the depth of this great love.

I leave you with Paul's prayer for the Ephesians:

For this reason I kneel before the Father, from whom every family in heaven and on earth derives its name. pray that out of his glorious riches he may strengthen you with power through his Spirit in your inner being, so that Christ may dwell in your hearts through faith. And I pray that you, being rooted and established in love, may have power, together with all the Lord's holy people, to grasp how wide and long and high and deep is the love of Christ, and to know this love that surpasses knowledge—that you may be filled to the measure of all the fullness of God.

– Ephesians 3:14-19

BOOKS FOR ENCOUNTERING FATHER'S LOVE

Brother Lawrence
- *Practicing the Presence of God*

Stephen Hill
- *You Deserve the Love of God*

Hannah Hurnard
- *Hinds Feet on High Places*

James Jordan
- *Sonship*
- *The Ancient Road Rediscovered*

Julian of Norwich
- *Revelations of Divine Love*

C.S. Lewis
- *The Great Divorce*
- *Surprised by Joy*

Brennan Manning
- *Abba's Child*

Andrew Murray
- *Absolute Surrender*

Henri Nouwen
- *Life of the Beloved*

- *The Return of the Prodigal Son*

Jim Wilder
- *Renovated: God, Dallas Willard and the Church that Transforms*

Dallas Willard
- *The Divine Conspiracy*
- *Hearing God*

HEALING MINISTRY RESOURCES

Love Inside Out
Raleigh, NC
www.loveinsideout.org

Fatherheart Ministries
Taupo, New Zealand
www.fatherheart.net

Gary and Lisa Black
Colorado Springs, CO
www.garyandlisablack.com

Restoring the Foundations
Mount Juliet, TN
www.restoringthefoundations.org

Christian Healing Ministries
Jacksonville, FL
www.christianhealingmin.org

ENDNOTES

Introduction: The Ugly Weed

1. Henri Nouwen, *The Return of the Prodigal Son* (New York: Doubleday, 1992), 95.

Chapter 1: Head Versus Heart

1. Henri Nouwen, *The Way of the Heart: The Spirituality of the Desert Fathers and Mothers* (San Francisco: HarperOne, 2009), 87.

2. C.S. Lewis, *Mere Christianity* (New York: Touchstone, 1996), 169.

Chapter 2: The Eyes of the Heart

1. James Jordan, *The Ancient Road Rediscovered* (Taupo, New Zealand: Fatherheart Media, 2014), 186-187.

2. C.S. Lewis, *Mere Christianity* (New York: Touchstone, 1996), 176.

Chapter 3: A Story of Surrender

1. Andrew Murray, "Ye are the Branches: An Address to Christian Workers."

Chapter 4: From Battling to Abiding

1. Henri Nouwen, *The Return of the Prodigal Son* (New York: Image, 1994), 37-38.

2. Andrew Murray, "Absolute Surrender."

Chapter 5: Big Fears, Little Fears

1. Henri Nouwen, *The Return of the Prodigal Son* (New York: Image, 1994), 121.

Chapter 6: The Most Excellent Way

1.   Emily P. Freeman, *The Next Right Thing* Podcast, Episode 94.

2.   Dallas Willard, *The Divine Conspiracy* (New York: Harper Collins, 1997), 183.

3.   Bob Goff, *Everybody Always* (Nashville: Nelson Books, 2018), 73.

4.   Jim Wilder, *Renovated* (Colorado Springs: NavPress, 2020), 86.

Chapter 7: Forgiveness is Key

1.   N.T. Wright, *Surprised by Hope: Rethinking Heaven, Resurrection, and the Mission of the Church* (San Francisco, HarperOne, 2008), 288.

2.   Henri Nouwen, *The Return of the Prodigal Son* (New York: Image, 1994), 75.

Chapter 8: Your True Identity

1.   Jim Wilder, *Renovated* (Colorado Springs: NavPress, 2020), 79.

2.   Maria Furlough, *Breaking the Fear Cycle* (Grand Rapids: Revell, 2018), 37.

3.   Henri Nouwen, *Bread for the Journey,* (San Francisco: HarperOne, 2009), 210.

Chapter 9: The Quality of Eternal Life

1.   C.S. Lewis, *Surprised by Joy* (London: Harcourt Brace, 1955), 72.

2.   Lewis, *Surprised by Joy*, 7.

3.   Andrew Murray, *Let Us Draw Nigh,* Chapter V, "With a True Heart."

Chapter 10: Receiving His Love

1. Julian of Norwich, *Revelations of Divine Love*, Chapter LXXIII.

2. Julian of Norwich, *Revelations of Divine Love*, Chapter V.

3. Dallas Willard, *Living in Christ's Presence: Final Words of Heaven and the Kingdom of God*, (Downers Grove: IVP, 2014), 56.

4. Andrew Murray, *With Christ in the School of Prayer* (New Kensington, PA: Whitaker House, 1981), 109-110.

5. Henri Nouwen, *The Return of the Prodigal Son* (New York: Image, 1994), 82.

6. Watchman Nee, *The Spiritual Man* (New York: Christian Fellowship Publishers, 2014), 184.

7. C.S. Lewis, *The Great Divorce* (San Francisco: HarperCollins, 2001), 100.

Chapter 11: Getting Practical

1. Dallas Willard, *Hearing God* (Downers Grove: IVP, 2012), 143.

2. Henri Nouwen, *The Return of the Prodigal Son* (New York: Image, 1994), 84.

Chapter 12: Living in the Spacious Place

1. Brother Lawrence, *The Practice of the Presence of God*, Sixth Letter.

L♦VE
INSIDE OUT